USEFUL REFERENCE SERIES No. 94

INDEX TO ONE ACT PLAYS

FIFTH SUPPLEMENT

1956-1964

AN INDEX TO

ONE-ACT PLAYS

for Stage, Radio, and Television

FIFTH SUPPLEMENT 1956-1964

By

HANNAH LOGASA

AUTHOR - BOOK SELECTION IN EDUCATION

BOSTON

F. W. FAXON COMPANY, INC.

1 9 6 6

LIBRARY OF CONGRESS CATALOG CARD NUMBER 24-21477

TABLE OF CONTENTS

PREFACE

The reason why this bibliography should be a useful reference book is because the volumes of one-act plays are not adequately catalogued in most libraries. The volume as a whole is included, but the individual plays in it do not appear. Moreover the classification scatters one-act play material in many places on the shelves, and they appear under various headings,—recreations; holidays; health; history; biography; religion; as well as in the literature of many countries; in special collections for children and adults. Thus finding an individual play in a library is an adventure.

Over one thousand plays are included in this supplement, in addition to the great number of duplicates that appear in more than one volume.

The number of one-act play collections available was disappointing. It would seem as though that medium of literary expression does not attract the number of writers it formerly did. However, we are fortunate that some of the earlier classic writers in the field have been reprinted in collections with a later copyright date, and are included in this supplement.

In the past, many one-act plays were written by outstanding authors as well as good craftsmen. The form was right for the unities of time, place and mood. The very shortness of the material as it treats a single incident or event lent itself to that unity. Such plays as "The Riders to the Sea", and many others provided a rich emotional experience.

Not many of the very recent plays observe the unities. They are influenced by television and the movie. Scenes are shifted from one place to another with rapidity, with little dialogue in each. This scene shifting takes away from the impression as a whole.

As always, there is a preponderance of plays for children. These are mostly on the subjects of Christmas, fairies, holidays, and the great characters in American history. Recently more plays have been written for the junior level. The subjects treated are mostly those also written for children with the addition of a few concerned with the special interests of the teen-agers. For both children and young people there are now a great number of plays that can be performed without royalty.

Scenes from well-known three-act plays have been made into one-act plays. The selection of a scene may not answer the criteria of a one-act play, but since they do so in form and content, they were included.

There are also a number of adaptations of novels. Scenes have been made into one-act plays. In this, it is much like what happened to the three-act plays. Since outstanding books were used, they enrich the field, and add variety to it.

Foreign writers are represented in this supplement. Here also, there are fewer one-act plays than formerly. The question may be asked whether the seeming lack of interest is not a general trend.

Play Magazine has contributed a great number of plays to this supplement. These are for children, and young people. Some of them have appeared before in collections, or as separates.

Both for radio, and television, there is a dearth of one-act plays that can be identified as such. This is especially true of television where one might expect to find a wealth of material in a relatively new field. However, this is not the case. Such plays as are available have been influenced by the screen technique, and are, in form not one-act plays. No matter how broad the basis for selection might be — few could be included.

A survey of the field of the one-act play would indicate that it is not as prolific as formerly. Few collections were published then in a comparable period.

I wish to thank the Library of Congress, and the Public Libraries in various cities for the opportunity of examining their drama collection, and for providing the facilities for me to analyze the material I found suitable for this purpose.

June, 1965.   Hannah Logasa.

ABBREVIATIONS

Adapt.	Adaptor, adaptation
Ann.	Announcer
b.	Boy character
c.	Suitable for children
Char.	Characters
com.	Comedy
Comp.	Compiler
ed.	Edited
ext.	Extras
g.	Girl character
Int.	Interior
J.	Juvenile
m.	Men characters
Nar.	Narrator
n.d.	No date
n-r.	Non royalty
r.	Radio
rm.	Room
sc.	Scene
t.	Television
V.	Voices
w.	Women characters

HOW TO USE THIS INDEX

The Key is the bibliographical identification of a play. Key letters refer to the book in which the play may be found; if a pamphlet separate, to the publisher responsible for its publication; to the magazine in which the play appeared.

The Title Index contains full information about each individual play, whether it is a radio, or television play; author; number and kind of characters; setting or background, — suitability for elementary, or high school pupils — followed by the key letters which show where the play is to be found.

Refer to the title index from the author, subject, and collections sections.

AN INDEX TO ONE-ACT PLAYS

KEY

A

AD   Adair, Margaret W. Do-it-in-a day puppets. N. Y. Day, 1964.
AG   Agee, James. On film. vol 2. N.Y. McDowell, 1960.
AN   Anderson, G. L. ed. Masterpieces of the Orient. N. Y. Norton, 1961.

B

BAC   Bacher, W. A. ed. Treasury star parade. N. Y. Farrar, 1942.
BAD   Bachman, J. W. & Browne, E. M. Better plays for today's churches. N. Y. Association, 1964.
BAK   Baker, Walter H. Co. 100 Summer St. Boston, Mass. Separates.
BAR   Barrie, J. M. Plays of J. M. Barrie. N. Y. Scribner, 1952.
BAS   Barry, Michael, ed. The television playright. N. Y. Hill & Wang, 1960.
BE   Becker, R. G. Plays for our time. N. Y. Oxford, 1959.
BEB   Beckett, Samuel. End game; Act without words. N. Y. Grove, 1958.
BEC   Beckett, Samuel. Krapp's last tape & other dramatic pieces. N. Y. Grove, 1960.
BEN   Benedict, Michael & Wellwarth, G. E. Modern French theater. N. Y. Dutton, 1964.
BF   Bentley, Eric, ed. From the modern repertoire, Ser. 3. Bloomington, Indiana Uni., 1956.
BOU4   Bourne, John, ed. New play annual for women. No. 4. London, Evans, 1959.
BOU7   Bourne, John, ed. New play annual for women. No. 7. London, Evans, 1963.
BR   Bridie, James. Tedious & brief. London, Constable. n.d.
BRB   Bright, F. F. & Potter, Ralph. To be an American. Phil. Lippincott, 1957.
BRC   Brings, L. M. ed. Clubwoman's entertainment book. Minneapolis, Denison, 1957.
BRG   Brings, L. M. ed. Gay nineties melodramas. Minneapolis, Denison, 1963.
BRH   Brings, L. M. ed. Golden book of Christmas plays. Minneapolis, Denison, 1962.
BRHM   Brings, L. M. comp. Master stunt book. Minneapolis, Denison, 1956.
BRI   Brings, L. M. ed. One-act dramas & contest plays. Minneapolis, Denison, 1962.
BRJ   Brings, L. M. ed. Rehearsal-less skits & plays. Minneapolis, Denison, 1963.

BRO   Brown, Regina. A play at your house. N. Y. Obolensky, 1962.

BRT   Browne, E. M. 21 medieval mystery & morality plays. N. Y. Meridan, 1958.

BUR   Burack, A. S. ed. Four-star plays for boys. Boston, Plays, 1957.

BUU   Burack, A. S. ed. Prize contest plays for young people. Boston, Plays, 1962.

BUW   Burack, A. S. ed. Treasury of holiday plays for teen-agers. Boston, Plays, 1963.

C

CAR   Carlson, Bernice W. Right play for you. N. Y. Abingdon, 1960.

CARR   Carroll, P. V. Irish stories & plays. N. Y. Devin-Adair, 1958.

CARS   Carver, C. H. and others. America today. Englewood Cliffs, N. J. Prentice-Hall, 1959.

CART   Carver, C. H. and others. They found adventure. Englewood Cliffs, N. J. Prentice-Hall, 1960.

CARV   Carver, C. H. and others. Youth & the future. Englewood Cliffs, N. J. Prentice-Hall, 1959.

CAS   Casey, Bernice M. Good things for Mother's Day. Minneapolis, Denison, 1960.

CAT   Casey, F. J. Staging the Bible. Westminister, Maryland, Newman. 1962.

CER   Cerf, Bennett & Cartwell, V. H. 24 favorite one-act plays. N. Y. Doubleday, 1958.

CI   Citron, S. J. ed. Dramatics the year round. N. Y. United Synagogue Congr. 1956.

CJ   Clapp, E. R. & others. College quad. N. Y. Dryden, 1956.

CLI   Clark, B. H. ed. World drama, N. Y. Dover, n.d. vol. 1.

CL2   Clark, B. H. ed. World drama, N. Y. Dover, n.d. vol. 2.

COO   Cook, Luella B. & Others. People in literature. N. Y. Harcourt, 1957.

COW   Coward, Noel. Collected plays. London, Heinamann, 1954.

D

DAL   Dale, Chalmers, ed. In the presence of death. St. Louis, Bethany, 1964.

DEC   Decker, R. G. ed. Plays for our time. N. Y. Oxford, 1959.

DIA   Dias, E. J. One-act plays for teen-agers. Boston, Plays, 1961.

DO   Downer, A. S. Art of the play. N. Y. Holt, 1955.

DRA   Dramatists Play Service. 14 East 38th. St. N. Y. Separates.

DUR   Durrell, Donald D. & Crossley, B. A. 30 plays for classroom reading. Boston, Plays, 1957.

E

EDM	Edades, Jean, ed. More short plays of the Philippines. Manila, Benipayo, 1957.
EDS	Edades, Jean, ed. Short plays of the Philippines, Benipayo, 1958.
EM	Emmons, Delia G. Northwest history in action. Minneapolis, Denison 1960.
EMM	Emurian, E. K. Ten new plays for church & school. Boston, Wilde 1959.
ES	Estes, Susan. In quest of power. Nashville, Broadman, 1954.
EV	Everard, Elizabeth, ed. Ten one-act plays for women. London, Harrap, 1958.

F

FEI	Feigenbaum, L. A. ed. Radio & television plays. N. Y. Globe, 1956.
FEL	Felheim, Marvin. Plays, theory & criticism. N. Y. Harcourt, 1962.
FEM	Fenga, I. & others. Pilot series in literature. Bk. I. Michigan, Grand Rapids, 1957.
FEN	Fenner, Phyllis & Hughes, Avah. Entrances & exits. N. Y. Dodd, 1960.
FIR	Fisher, Eileen. Christmas plays & programs. Boston, Plays, 1960.
FIS	Fisher, Eileen. Patriotic plays & programs. Boston, Plays, 1956.
FIT	Fisher, Eileen. Plays about our nation's songs. Boston, Plays, 1962.
FIU	Fisher, Eileen. U N plays & programs. Boston, Plays, 1965.
FL	Florentino, A. S. ed. Outstanding Filipino short plays. Manila, Filipinana, 1961.
FQ	Free Company. Collection of plays about the meaning of Amercia. N. Y. Dodd, 1941.
FR	French, Samuel, inc. 25 W. 25th St. N. Y. Separates.
FRY	Fry, Christopher. Three plays. N. Y. Oxford, 1961.

G

GP	Graham, C. B. ed. Freshman English program. Chic. Scott Foresman, 1960.
GR	Green, Paul. Five plays of the South. N. Y. Hill & Wang, 1963.
GUD	Guder, Eileen L. What happened after . . . Los Angeles, Cowman, 1962.
GUN	Gunn, John. ed. Seeking years. St. Louis, Bethany, 1959.

H

HAL1 Halverson, Marvin. Religious dramas No. 1. N. Y. Meridian, 1957.

HAL2 Halverson, Marvin. Religious dramas No. 3. N. Y. Meridian, 1959.

HAR Hark, Mildred & McQueen, Noel. Special plays for special days. Boston, Plays, 1960.

HAT Hark, Mildred & McQueen, Noel. Teen age plays for all occasions. Boston, Plays, 1957.

HAV Havinghurst, Walter & others. Selection. N. Y. Dryden, 1955.

HAY Hayes, Richard. Port Royal & other plays. N. Y. Hill & Wang, 1962.

HI Holbrook, David, comp. Thieves & angels. London, Cambridge Uni. 1962.

HLM Hook, J. N. & others. Literature of adventure. Boston, Ginn, 1957.

HN Hopper, V. F. & Lahey, G. B. ed. Medieval mystery plays. N. Y. Barron, 1962.

HO Housman, Lawrence. Gracious Majesty. N. Y. Scribner, 1957.

HOW Howard, Vernon, comp. Short plays from the great classics. London, Sterling, 1960.

HU Huber, L. J. Humorous acts for stunt programs. Minneapolis, Denison, 1963.

HUB Huberman, Edward & Raymo, R. R. Angles of vision. Boston, Houghton, 1962.

I

IN Inge, William. Summer brave & eleven short plays. N. Y. Random, 1962.

IV Iverson, W. J. & McCarthy, Agnes L. Prose & poetry journeys, 5th ed. Syracuse N. Y. Singer, 1957.

J

JA Jagendorf, Moritz, ed. 20 non-royalty one-act ghost plays. N. Y. Greenberg, 1946.

JN John, Gwen. Plays. London, Duckworth, n.d.

JO Johnson, Crane. Past sixty. San Francisco, International, 1953.

JOH Johnson, Denis. The old lady says "no" & other plays. Boston, Atlantic, 1961.

K

KAM Kamerman, Sylvia E. ed. Blue-ribbon plays for graduation. Boston, Plays, 1957.

KAN Kamerman, Sylvia E. ed. Treasury of Christmas plays. Boston, Plays, 1958.

KIR   Kissen, Fan. Golden Goose & other plays. Boston, Houghton, 1963.

KIS   Kissen, Fan. They helped make America. Boston, Houghton, 1958.

KO   Konick, Marcus, ed. Plays for modern youth. N. Y. Globe, 1961.

KR   Krige, Uys. The sniper & other one-act plays. Capetown, Pretoria, 1962.

L

LAU   Lauder, Sister M. Genevieve. Plays for grade & high school children. N. Y. Exposition, 1956.

LO   Long, W. I. Twelve half-hours with the Winthrop theatre. Rock Hill, So. Carolina, Winthrop College, 1959.

Mc

MCB   McCaslin, Nellie. Pioneers in petticoats. Evanston, Row Peterson, 1960.

MCC   McCaslin, Nellie. Tall tales & tall men. Philadelphia, Macrae, 1956.

MCJ   McCoy, P. S. Just for variety. Evanston, Row Paterson, 1958.

MCO   McCoy, P. S. Modern comedies for teen-agers. Boston, Plays, 1962.

MCR   McCrae, Lillian. Puppets & puppet plays. London, Oxford, 1952.

MCS   McKellar, H. D. Beyond the footlights. Toronto, Macmillan, 1963.

M

MA   Macneice, Louis. Mad island & the administrator. London, Faber, 1964.

MA1   Mayorga, Margaret. Best short plays of 1955-56. Boston, Beacon, 1957.

MA2   Mayorga, Margaret. Best short plays of 1956-57. Boston, Beacon, 1958.

MA3   Mayorga, Margaret. Best short plays of 1957-58. Boston, Beacon, 1959.

MA4   Mayorga, Margaret. Best short plays of 1959-1960. Boston, Beacon, 1961.

MA5   Mayorga, Margaret. Best short plays of 1960-61. Boston, Beacon, 1962.

MAL   Malcolmson, Anne. Miracle plays. Boston, Houghton, 1959.

MAU   Maugham, W. S. Encore. N. Y. Doubleday, 1952.

MH   Miksch, W. F. Teen-age comedies. Minneapolis, Denison, 1962.

MIE   Miller, Helen L. Easy plays for boys and girls. Boston, Plays, 1963.

MIF   Miller, Helen L.   First plays for children.   Boston, Plays, 1960.

MIG   Miller, Helen L.   Gold medal plays for holidays.   Boston, Plays, 1960.

MIL   Miller, Helen L.   Modern plays for special days.   Boston, Plays, 1965.

MIZ   Miller, Sarah W.   Acting out the truth.   Nashville, Broadman, 1961.

MOD   —— Modern short skits & stunt book.   Minneapolis, Denison, 1963.

MON   Montano, Severino. ed.   Prize winning plays of the Arena theatre of the Philippines.   Quezon City, Phoenix, 1958.

MOO   Moon, Samuel.   One act.   N. Y. Grove, 1961.

MU   Murray, John.   Comedies & farces for teen-agers.   Boston, Plays, 1959.

MUC   Murray, John.   Comedy round-up for teen-age actors.   Boston, Plays, 1964.

MUR   Murray, John.   One-act plays for young actors.   Minneapolis, Denison, 1959.

N

NE   Neville, M. A. & Herzberg, M. J. Literature in America.   Chicago, Rand McNally, 1958.

NEV   New Directions.   Playbook.   Norfolk, Conn., 1956.

NEW   Newman, Deborah.   Holiday plays for little players.   Boston, Plays, 1957.

NO   Nolan, P. T.   Round-the-world plays for young people.   Boston, Plays, 1961.

O

OC   O'Casey, Sean.   Three plays.   N. Y. St. Martins, 1961.

OK   Okun, Lillian.   Let's listen to a story.   N. Y. Wilson, 1959.

OLI   Olfson, Lewy, ed.   Dramatized classics for radio-style reading.   Vol. I. Boston, Plays, 1964.

ON   O'Neil, Eugene.   Ten lost plays.   N. Y. Random, 1964.

OS   Osborne, John.   Plays for England.   London, Faber, 1963.

P

PE   Pethybridge, D. C.   Directed drama.   London, Uni. of London, 1951.

PHI   Phillips, J. B.   Man called Jesus.   N. Y. Macmillan, 1959.

PLA   Plays Magazine.   Vol. 22.   Oct.-May, 1962-1963.

PLAY   Plays, Inc.   8 Arlington St., Boston.   Separates.

POE   Pooley R. C. & others.   Exploring life through literature, Chicago, Scott Foresman, 1957.

POG   Pooley R. C. & others.   Good times through literature.   Chicago, Scott Foresman, 1957.

POO   Pooley, R. C. & others. Wide, wide world. Chicago, Scott Foresman, 1959.

POW   Powers, V. E. ed. Nights of Noel. Evanston, Ill., Row Peterson, 1959.

POX   Powers, V. E. ed. Plays for players. Evanston, Ill., Row Peterson, 1957.

PR   Pratt, Lois H. Puppet do-it-yourself book. N. Y. Exposition, 1957.

Q

QU   Quinlan, M. Eva. Plays for early teens. N. Y. Baker, 1948.

R

RED   Rees, Leslie, ed. Mask & microphone. Sydney, Australia, 1963.

REE   Reeves, James. Peddler's dream & other plays. N. Y. Dutton, 1963.

REH   Reinert, Otto. Drama. Boston, Little Brown, 1961.

RIC   Reines, Bernard J. For country & mankind. N. Y. Longmans 1954.

REI   Richardson, Willis. King's dilemma & other plays for children. N. Y. Exposition, 1956.

S

SAI   St. Clair, Robert. Religious plays for amateur players. Minneapolis, Denison, 1964.

SAN   Sando, Esther G. Pair of gloves. Philadelphia, Christian Education, 1962.

SAR   Sartoris, Roman. Three plays. N. Y. Black Sun, 1944.

SCH   Schneideman, Rose. Radio plays for young people to act. N. Y. Dutton, 1961.

SCHR   Schramm, Wilbur & others. Adventure for Americans. N. Y. Harcourt, 1956.

SEF   Segal, S. M. On stage everyone. N. Y. Jonathen David, 1957.

SER   Serling, Rod. Patterns. N. Y. Simon & Schuster, 1957.

SET   Settel, Irving. Best television humor of the year. N. Y. Wyn, 1956.

SH   Shaw, Bernard. Seven one-act plays. Baltimore, Penguin, 1958.

SHA   Shaw, Bernard. The shorter plays. N. Y. Dodd Mead, 1960.

SL   Sloane, Gertrude L. Fun with folktales. N. Y. Dutton, 1952.

SM   Smith, M. R. Plays & how to put them on. N. Y. Walck, 1961.

SMI   Smith, R. G. Boy's entertainment book. Minneapolis, Denison, 1957.

SO   Somerscales, Marjorie T. Fourteen short plays for young players. London, Pitman, 1962.

SP   Spark, Muriel. Voices at play. Philadelphia, Lippincott, 1962.

ST   Strindberg, August. Five plays of Strindberg. N. Y. Doubleday, 1960.

T

TI   Tichenor, Tom. Folk plays for puppets you can make. Nashville, Abington 1959.

TU   Turgenev, Ivan. Three famous plays. N. Y. Hill & Wang, 1959.

U

UL   Ulanov, Barry. Makers of the modern drama. N. Y. McGraw-Hill, 1961.

V

VE   Very, Alice. Round the clock plays for children. Boston, Plays, 1957.

W

WAL   Wallerstein, J. S. Adventure, five plays for youth. N. Y. Bellamy, 1956.

WAR   Ward, R. H. ed. Ten peace plays. London, Dent n. d.

WE   Weiss, S. A. Drama in the modern world. Boston, Heath 1964.

WIL   Wilde, Percival. Comrad in arms. Boston, Baker n. d.

WH   Williams, Charles. Collected plays. London, Oxford, 1963.

Z

ZA   Zachar, I. J. Plays as experience. Rev. N. Y. Odyssey, 1963.

TITLE INDEX

A

c n–r	ABC's Thanksgiving (Miller) 3b 2g extras. sc. stage. MIE
c n–r	Abe Lincoln & little Joe (Hark) 12b 2g sc. backdrop HAR.
c n–r	Abe Lincoln goes to school. (Very) 5b Ig sc. cabin. VE
	Abe Lincoln in Illinois (Sherwood) 3m extras sc. R.R. station. NE
	Abortion (O'Neil) 4m 3w extras. sc. dormitory of university ON
R	Above suspicion (Anderson) 3m 2w sc. int. FQ
	Abraham & Isaac (————) 4m. sc. medieval int. HL
	Abraham & Isaac (————) 2m. sc. curtains HN
	Abraham & Isaac (Housman) Im Iw Ib. sc. tent. BAD
J	Abraham & Isaac (Malcolmson) 4b. sc. 4sc. outdoors. MAL
c	Abraham Lincoln (Kissen) 8b Ig sc office. KIS
	Abstractions (————) Im 2w sc Japanese int. CLI
	Accident of birth (Fisher) 4m 2w sc. stage FIU
	Achosh Veros, incorporated (Segal) 8 roles sc. office. SEF SEG
	Acid test (Smith) 2w sc Sitting rm. BAK
	Act without words (Beckett) Im sc desert BEC
	Act without words (Beckett) II 2 characters sc platform BEB
c	Adalimina's pearl (Asbrand) Nar ib 3g Sc. outdoors DUR
	Adam (————) 8 m Iw sc paradise CLI
	Adam's rib hurts (Kilpatrick) 2m 6w sc. int. FR
R	Administrator (Macneice) 10m 3w sc dream MA
T	Admiral (Mac Leish) Nar. Ib Sc. ocean BRB
	Admirable Bashville (Shaw) 9m 2w sc glade in a park. SH
J	Admiral's nightmare (McGowan) 9b 3g extras sc ship. PLA MIE
c	Adobe Christmas (Peterson) 3b 3g sc. int. KAN
T	Adventure of Ozzie & Harriet (Nelson) 4m 2w Sc television SET
c	Adventure of Tom Sawyer (Brown) Nar. 3b 2g sc int. BRO
c	Aesop, man of fables (Phillips) 7b Ig sc stage PLA
J	Affair in the park (Miksch) 3b sc bench in a park MH
	Affair of dishonor (Wilde) 5m. sc English int WH
	African queen (Agee) 4m 4w voices sc African village AG
	After the ball (McCoy) 3m 4w sc int MOD
J	Afternoon at Central station (Miksch) 5b 2g extras sc. R.R. station
	Afterwards (McGanghan) 3m Iw sc Int. FR
	Agustina of the light heart (Mack) 4m Iw sc train EDS
	Ah, romance (Hackett) 8w sc Old ladies home BAK
T	Airmail from Cyprus (Hall) 4w 2m Sc. Hallway. BAS
n–r	Alabaster cruse (Miller) 7m 3w extras FR

19

c n–r   Aladdin (Newman) 4b 5g extras sc home NEW
J n–r   Aladdin steps out (Hark) 10b 4g sc int. HAT
          Albuquerque ten minutes (Ryerson) 2m 3w sc R.R. station. FR
          Alcestis (Euripides) 6m Iw chorus sc Royal house GLI
          Alcestis (Euripides) 6m 2w Chorus sc palace in ancient Greece
              RED
c   Ali Baba & the 40 thieves (Felsbein) Nar. 6b Ig sc. Arabian int.
              DUR
c   Ali Baba & the 40 thieves (Klein) 14b 7g Nar. sc. stage. FEN
c   Alice in bookland (Urban) 2b 3g sc stage PLA
          Alice in puzzleland (Fisher) 4b 2g sc wood. FIU
J   Alice in Queenland (Follen) Any number of girls sc. curtains
              BAK
J n–r   Alice in wonderland (Carroll) Nar 16 characters sc river OLI
              PLA
J   All aboard for Christmas (Hark) 4b 4g sc. int. HAT
c R   All alone (Bishop) 5b sc int OK
c n–r   All American tour (Newman) Nar 15 characters extras sc Air-
              plane. NEW
          All in a day's work (Guder) 4m 1w sc Magistrate's office GUD
          All in the UN (Fisher) 2b 1g extras sc int. F1U
J   All out for Halloween (Hark) 5m 2b 2g sc. int. BAK
          All quiet in the air (Russell) 4m 3w voices sc underground WAR
          All roads lead to Rome (Krige) 7m 3w 1c sc. Village square KR
R   All that fall (Beckett) 6m 3w 1b voice Sc Old house BEC WE
          All the world around (Fisher) Nar 7m 3w sc stage F1U
c   All the world loves a mother (Casey) 14b sc outdoors CAS
J n–r   All this & Alan, too (Sanders) 5g sc dormitory BUU
J   All who enter (Huber) 1m 2w sc school office BRR
c J T   Almanac of liberty (Rose) 6b 6g extras sc Street DEC CARS
c n–r   Aloha, mother (Miller) 5b 7g sc classroom MIE
c   Aloysius bigmouth (Smith) 3b extras sc meeting place SMI
c   Altogether! Heave! (Carlson) 6b. extras sc country road CAR
J n–r   America is song (Nolan) 11b 3g sc wagon-train camp NO PLA
R   American crusader (Sherwood) 4m 2w sc int FQ
R   American names (Nurnberg) Nar 8b sc Immigration office HN
          Amicable parting (Kaufman) 1m 1w 1dog sc int DRA
          Among the faithless (Bayot) 9m 2w sc open field FL
T   Amorous goldfish (Voysey) Many characters & scenes sc court
              BAS
          And a song was born (Marston) 6m 4w sc int FR
J n–r   And Christmas is its name (Nolan) 16b 9g sc stage NO
          And he came to his father (Kruckemeyer) 4m 2w extras sc int
              FR
J   And lose his soul (St Clair) 2b 2g sc int SAI
          And there was light (Nappier) 2m 3w sc int LO
          And what a rummage sale (Kaser) 12w sc. store BAK

Angel of the battlefield (McCaslin) 8m 10w sc farmhouse MCB

Angry sea (Tabunar) 3m 3w sc. sea EDM

R   Ann Rutledge (Corwin) Nar 3m 7w voices sc. int BE DEC

Annajouska, the Bolshevik Empress (Shaw) 3m 1w sc military camp SHA

J   Anonymous letter (Fisher) 2b 2g sc int FIS

Answer (Freeman) 7m 1w sc int. FR

R   Answering the call (Emmons) 16b 5g extras sc church EM

J   Ant & the grasshoppers (Maugham) 7m 7w sc garden MAU

Antic spring (Nall) 3m 3w sc open touring car FR

Antigone (Sophocles) 7m 3w chorus sc. before royal palace CLI HAV UL

Anti-gossip club (Palmer) 10w sc. int BAK

J   Anybody's gift (Miksch) 3b 3g sc int MH

J   Anyone for the moon– (Alderman) 7b 3g sc office on the moon BUU

Anything to get the votes (Drummond) 6w sc int BRC

c   Anywhere & everywhere (Boiko) any number of characters sc earth PLA

Apollo of Bellac (Valeney) 9, 3w sc business office FR CER

c   Apple of discord (Oller) 3b 3g sc in ancient Greece POG

Apple-pie order (Morris) 8w sc room in palace EV

c J   Apples in the wilderness (McCaslin) 10b 5g extras sc orchard MCC

J   Apostle of freedom (Fisher) 3b 2g sc Colonial home FIS

Architruc (Pinget) 4m sc int BEN

Archy & Mehitabel (Kleinsinger) Any number of characters. sc office MA2

J   Around the world—by way of America (Howard) Nar 9b 1g 3c extras sc R.R. car HOW

Arrest (The) (Krige) 1m 7w sc homestead in Africa KR

c J   Arrest in the garden (Phillips) 6b 2g sc garden PHI

Arrival in person (McCoy) 2m 2w sc int. MOD

J   Art alliance (Miksch) 2b 2g sc outdoors MH

Art is a wonderful thing (McCoy) 3w sc art gallery MOD

c   Arthur's sword (Smith) 10b 6g sc Medieval tournament SM

As moths unto the lamp (Watts) 5w sc int BAK

As silent as the ocean (Manning) 1m 2w sc int LO

J   As we forgive (St Claire) 4b 2g sc int SAI

c   Ascension (Phillips) 7b sc hillside PHI

Ascension (York) 3m 1w sc outdoors BRT

Asher, the camel boy (Sando) Any number of characters. sc outside SAN

J   Ask Mr. Jefferson (Fisher) 3b 2g sc stage FIS

Astonished heart (Coward) 4m 3w int COW

Astonishing Mrs. O'Shaugnessey (Johnson) 3m 1w sc Art museum JO

C n–r   **Bashful bunny** (Miller) 3b 3g sc woods MIG

c n–r   **Baskets or bonnets** (Miller) 8b 17g extras sc park MIE

J   **Battle of the budget** (Martens) 4b 4g sc int BAK

   Battle of wits (Williams) 4m 2w sc stage FR

   Bauble for the baby (Conkle) 1m 3w sc int FR

   Be careful, judge (Huber) 3m 3w extras com sc int HU

J   **Be nice to the Easter bunny** (Martens) 5b 5g extras sc stage BAK

   Be not afraid (Citron) Nar 1b 1g voice sc int CI

c   **Be prepared** (Smith) nar 2b 2g sc int SMI

   Beacon of strength (Brenner) 3w 5g extras sc outdoors BAK

J n–r   **Beatnik & the Bard** (Dias) 3b 4g com sc office DIA

J   **Beauty parade** (Seiler) 10b 4g farce sc curtains DRA

   Beauty is fled (Carroll) 6m 2w extras sc workshop in Europe CARR

   Bedtime story (O'Casey) 4m 3w Burlesque sc int MOO

   Before the flood (Milne) 5m 5w sc ancient ark FR

   Behold the body (Federspual) 3m 4w com sc int LO

   Bell (The) (Housman) 1m 1w sc within the palace HO

   Bell of St. Hildegarde (Quinn) 8m 5w extras sc church FR

c j   **Bell witch of Tennessee** (McCaslin) 4b 5g extras sc home MCC

J   **Belles of Horsefly Gulch** (Murray) 7b 4g Melodrama sc cabin MUC

c   **Ben Franklin, peace-maker** (Howard) Nar 3b 1g sc. early American int DUR

J   **Benjamin Franklin** (Kissen) Nar 16b 3g extras sc stage KIS

   Bent fender (Huber) 2m 2w com sc automobile HU

   Bespoke overcoat (Mankowitz) 4m sc int FR

   Bessie, the bandit's beautiful baby (Price) 4m 5w com sc. int BRG

   Best bargain in the world (Fisher) 3m 2w sc int FIU

J R   **Best citizens of our town** (Schneideman) Ann 8b 5g sc int SCH

c n–r   **Best part of Christmas** (Newman) Nar 18 characters sc stage NEW

   Best way to die (Wong) 7m sc park EDS

c   **Betty & her friends** (McCrea) 2b 4g puppet sc int MCR

c   **Betty's birthday** (McCrea) 2b 4g puppet sc int MCR

c   **Betty's surprise** (McCrea) 2b 4g puppet sc int MCR

   Beware, Miss Brown, beware (Chambers) 2w sc int BRC

   Big business (McCoy) 2m 1w sc business office MOD

J   **Big hunt** (Miksch) 2b 3g sc. com inside automobile MH

J   **Bill, the matchmaker** (Drummond) 2b 2g com sc int BRRJ BRHM

J T   **Billy Adams, American** (Case) 10b 4g sc park KON

   Bilora (Beolco) 3m 2w sc street in medieval Italy CL2

   Bird in the bush (Martens) 1m 4w com sc field BAK

   Bird-catcher in hell (——) 2m extras chorus sc hell HL

c	Broken broomstick (Miller) 5b 3g sc clearing in the woods MIF
c J	Brother Sam (Herman) 7b sc stage CI
	Brown man's burden (Carino) 4m extras sc barber shop EDM
	Browning version (Rattingan) 5m 2w sc English school CER
	Brave new banner (McCaslin) Storyteller 3m 4w sc home in 1776 MCB
J	Bread (Eastman) 1b 4g sc farm home KON RR
	Bread of life (Casey) Nar 5m extras sc stage CAT
R	Bride comes to yellow sky (Agee) 4m 2w voices sc backwoods home AG
J n–r	Briefly speaking (McCoy) 2b 2g com sc reception rm MCO
	Bright is tomorrow (Nagel) 5w sc int BAK
	Brighten every corner (Herman) 6m 8w sc stage FR
J	Bringing up father (Fisher) 3m 3w sc int FIS
J n–r	Broomstick beauty (Miller) 2b 4g sc int BUW
J	Buddy buys an orchid (McMullen) 2b 3g com sc int BAK
c n–r	Bunch of keys (Hark) 3b 3g sc library HAR
	Bundles for Christmas (Harper) 9w sc int BAK
c n–r	Bunnies & bonnets (Miller) 6b 6g sc television studio MIG
	Bunny of the year (Newman) 4b 2g extras sc garden NEW
c	Burning schoolhouse (Smith) 7 characters sc outside schoolhouse SMI
	Bus Riley's back in town (Inge) 4m 2w sc fiesta rm IN
	Bus stops at Cactus Junction (McCoy) 7m 4w sc bus station MOD
c	Bus barbers (Miller) 14b 13g sc barber shop MIF
R J	By the dawn's early light (Cameron) Announcer 6b sc radio studio FEM
	By your hand (Huber) 4w sc int BRC HU

C

J n–r	Cabana blues (Hark) 4b 3g sc. school assembly hall HAT
	Cabbages (Standt) 3m 4w com sc New home FR
J c	Cactus wild cat (Wallerstein) 8b 4g sc western int BAK WAL
	Cadaver (Florentine) 2m 1w sc Philippino office EDM
	Cafe moon (Dunphy) 7m 2w sc cafe DRA
T	Call me a liar (Mortimer) 7m 6w sc boarding house BAS
	Call me dear (Huber) 3m 3w com sc int HU
J	Call Washington 1776 (Miller) 7b 7g sc int MIL
c n–r	Callers (The) (Very) 2b 4g sc int VE
R n–r	Calling all Christmases (Fisher) master of ceremonies 5b 5g sc radio FIR
c J	Calling of the disciples (Phillips) 3b sc outdoors in Palestine PHI
c	Camp Crowhill here we come (Miksch) 4b 3g com sc camp MH
c	Camp Ghost (Boretz) 2m 8b sc camp JA

	Child of peace (Willis) 2 narrators any number of characters sc church BAK
	Children of the Book (Miller) 13m 10w extras sc stage FR
J	**Children's Christmas pageant** (St. Clair) Nar any number of children sc church SAI
c	**China-handled knife** (Conkle) 10 char sc. schoolroom FR
c n–r	**Chosen one** (Duvall) 7b 3g sc French int KAN
	Christ enters Jerusalem (Phillips) 8b voices sc on a road PHI
	Christ in Concrete city (Turner) 4m 2w sc stage BAD
c	**Christ the son of God** (Phillips) 5b sc outdoors PHI
n–r	**Christmas apple** (Williams) 5m 6w sc int FR
	Christmas at check point Charlie (Felton) 3m Iw Ig sc Berlin wall BAK
	Christmas at mother's (Curtis) 3m 7w sc int BRH
c	**Christmas at the Cratchits** (Newman) 4b 4g sc home in London NEW
	Christmas at the Gables (Moore) 6w com sc int FR
	Christmas awakening (Cutler) 4m 3w sc stage BRH
	Christmas barricade (McCoy) 4m 4w sc lunch rm BRH
J n–r	**Christmas bug** (Larson) 1b 5g sc tea rm KAN
J	**Christmas candle** (St. Clair) Nar 3b Iw Ic sc int SAI
c J	**Christmas carol** (Dickens) any number of characters sc int BAK FR KAN PLA
J n–r	**Christmas coast to coast** (Olfson) 9b 4g extras sc int BUW
J n–r	**Christmas cowboy** (Miller) 4b 4g extras sc sun porch BUW
	Christmas eve dream (Shively) 6m 2w sc int BRH
c n–r	**Christmas eve letter** (Hark) 3b 4g extras sc int HAR
R J	**Christmas every day** (McGowan) 21 characters announcer sc int KAN
J n–r	**Christmas for Cosette** (Hugo) Nar 6b 3g sc French int OLI
	Christmas gift (Barbee) 4m 6w sc sun rm BRH
c n–r	**Christmas in court** (Fisher) 4b 3g sc stage FIR PLA
J n–r	**Christmas in quarantine** (Fisher) 2b 2g sc int FIR
	Christmas in the market place (Gheon) 2m 2w sc stage BAD
	Christmas in the Mountain Chapel (Lauder) large number char. sc chapel LAU
	Christmas incorporated (Kerr) 7w sc int FR
c	**Christmas inside** (Fletcher) any number of char sc int BAK
	Christmas is a racket (Cook) 2m 4w sc int BAK
R	**Christmas letter** (Mann) Announcer Im 2w sc radio BAC
	Christmas miracle (McDonald) 5m 5w sc int BRH
J	**Christmas nutcracker** (Thane) 9b 4g sc German village PLA
	Christmas on main street (Draper) 2m 2w extras sc int FR
J n–r	**Christmas recaptured** (Hark) 4b 4g sc int HAT
	Christmas rose (Phelps) 4m 4w com sc int BRH
c n–r	**Christmas runaways** (Miller) 4b 2g sc stable MIG
c n–r	**Christmas sampler** (Leuser) 6b 4g sc kitchen KAN

C J   Christmas spelldown (Fisher) 10 characters sc school FIR
J n–r   Christmas spirit (Dias) 4b 4g sc int DIA KAN
n–r   Christmas star for Olga (Webb) 7w sc int FR
           Christmas stranger (Emery) Im 3w sc int FR
c J   Christmas tablecloth (Fisher) 2b 3g sc int FIR
           Christmas that bounced (Johnson) 2m 5w sc int BRH
c n–r   Christmas tree surprise (Newman) 3b 3g extras sc outdoors
               NEW
c n–r   Christmas umbrella (Miller) 7b 7g sc. Santa's workshop MIG
           Christo (El) (Larkin) 4m 2w sc. Mexican home FR
J n–r   Cicero the great (McCoy) 2b Ig com sc int MCO
           Circle beyond fear (Swann) 6m 6w sc church BAD
           Circus story (Salacrou) 10m 1w extras sc tent of circus BEN
c   City mouse & country mouse (Tichenor) 7b puppet sc stage TI
           City slicker & our Nell (Price) 4m 5w sc "settin rm" com BGG
J   Citizen Franklin of Philadelphia (Reines) 7b 4g extras sc. int
               REI
c J   Clara Barton (Kissen) 14b 6g field of battle KIS
J   Clara Barton, lady of mercy (Reines) 12b 3g sc office REI
           Clean hands (Huber) 3m Iw com sc kitchen HU
J n–r   Cleanest town in the west (Dias) 6b 6g sc western dining rm
               DIA
c   Cleansing of the Temple (Phillips) 3b sc courtyard of the
               Temple PHI
           Cleopatra, the second (Drummond) 10w sc int BRC
J   Clock that rested (Segal) 12 children sc large clock SEF SEG
           Clock shop (Golden) 7 char extras sc int FR
           Clod (Beach) 4m 5w sc kitchen FR
           Clouds (The) (Aristophanes) 9m chorus sc ancient Athens CLI
           Clue to the wrong thing (Sartoris) 5m sc a path SAR
c   Coach (The) (Casey) 4b 6g sc int CAS
c n–r   Cock & the fox (Very) 3b 4g sc outdoors VE
           Cold face—warm heart (McCaslin) storyteller 2m 2w sc Indian
               village MCB
J   Collector's item (Dias) 4b 3g sc int PLA
J R   Colossal, Stupendous (Murray) 6b 3g sc com movie MU
           Come down (Sando) 7m Iw sc home in Jerusalem SAN
           Come over to Macedonia (Miller) 4m 3w sc church MIZ
J R   Coming of the Prince (McCowan) Nar 18 characters voice sc
               radio KAN
T   Command decision (Haines) 6m sc television BE
J   Command decision (Laidlaw) 5m sc battle field DEC
c   Compass for Columbus (Newman) 6b 4g sc harbor in Genoa
               NEW
           Competition (Huber) 3m 2w com sc farmhouse HU
c J   Comrad justice (Smith) 6b sc courtroom SMI
c J   Comrads all (Kabakoff) 10 characters sc int CI

Comrades in arms (Wilde) 2m 2w com sc int WH

Conspirators (The) (Carroll) 2m 1w sc in Ireland CARR

Contest by two (McCoy) 1m 1w com sc int MOD

n–r Cool yule (Coulter) 6g com sc int BAK

Corinna (John) 5m 7w Sc English int JN

J Corsair (The) (Somerscales) 12b pirate ship SO

J Costly gold hunt (Emmons) 9b 1g extras sc western mine EM

J Count of donkey's island (Folles) any number of boys sc farm-house BAK

n–r Counting the calories (McMullen) 6w com sc int BAK

Country auction (Farrar) 7m 4w extras com sc outdoors BAK

c Country store cat (Miller) 15b 6g extras sc country store MIF

Court, a Queen & the Church (Lauder) large number of char sc stage LAU

J n–r Courters (Noan) 5b 1g sc city square in Italy NO PLA

Cowards die a thousand deaths (Sicam) 4m sc tent EDM

Cow-catcher on the caboose (Devany) 6m 1w sc railroad MA3

J Craftsman, W. F. (Miksch) 3b 2g sc int MH

Create in me a clean heart, O God (Miller) 2 readers, chorus, 1m ext sc church MIZ

Creation of man (——) 1m extras sc heaven BRT

Creation of the heavenly beings (——) 4m sc heaven BRT

Creation sings the glory of God (Casey) Nar 4 singers choir sc stage CAT

Creditors (Strindberg) 2m 1w ext sc hotel in Sweden SP ST

Cretan woman (Jeffers) 3m 3w ext sc in ancient Greece BF

J Crime club (Sheldon) Announcer 4b sc stage BRJ

c Crimson feather (Watts) 6b 4g sc kitchen PLA

Cristina goes with goats (Mack) 2m 1w sc house in the Philippines EDS

Cross (The) (Miller) 4 readers 5m 1w sc church MIZ

c Crosspatch & cupid (Miller) 7b 6g sc classrm MIG

J R Crossroads to education (Schneideman) Announcer 4b 2g ext sc school SCH

Crucifixion (York) 4m 1w sc church BRT

J n–r Cry witch (Miller) 7b 7g sc meeting house in Salem BUU

c Crying clown (Nicholson) 4b sc outside circus tent BUR

J n–r Cuckoo (The) (Murdock) 7b sc int BUU

Cup of strength (Drake) 6w 1g sc shack BAK

J n–r Cupid & Co. (Callaman) 4b 4g sc office BUW

Curate's play (Banks) Nar 4m 2w 11b 1g sc. platform in church BAD

J n–r Curse of Hag Hollow (Miller) 2b 4g sc cave MIL

Curtain (Clemens) 1m 2w com sc int FR

Curtain capers (McCoy) 5m 1w orchestra sc curtains MCJ

Curtain time (Drummond) 2m 2w sc court BRHM

Cynthia (Brenner) 5w sc int BAK

D

Desert shall rejoice (Finch) 7m 2w sc Nevada desert FR

Desperate Desmond's dastardly deed (Price) 3m 6w Ic com sc int BRG

J   Devil & Daniel Webster (Benet) 6m 12 jurymen sc int CER DRA ZA

J n–r   Dial M for murder (Miller) 5b 3g sc int MIL

c   Dick Whittington (Lewis) 11b 4g sc int in London FEN

Diet begins tomorrow (Stearns) 5w com sc int BAK

n–r   Dilly dehaunting agency (Taylor) 5m 2w sc office JA

Dinner with the folks (Hark) 3m 2w sc int BAK

J   Dish of green peas (Fisher) 3b 2g sc colonial kitchen FIS

Distant thunder (Neuenburg) 4w sc int BAK

J   District school at Carrot Corners (Drummond) teacher 5b 5g com sc school BRJ

Divine spark (Curtis) 7w sc int BRC

Divorce is granted (Carmichael) 7w com sc int BAK

J   Do I bother you? (Huber) 2b 2g com sc int BRJ

Doctor decides (Eastman) 3m 3w sc int FR

c   Dog for Betty (McCrae) Nar 2b 4g puppets sc int MCR

Dog tricks (McCoy) 2m Iw com sc int MOD

c n–r   Dolly saves the day (Miller) 4b 2g sc old well MIG

Domestic difference (Housman) 3m 2w Sc. palace HO

J   Don Quixote saves the day (Cervantes) Nar 9b 4g ext sc country road HOW

J   Don't call me "Junior" (Bannick) 5b 4g com sc int BAK

J   Don't call us—we'll call you (Murray) 6b 3g com sc boarding house MUC

Don't cry, baby (Huber) 1m 3w com sc int HU

Don't get excited (Provence) 2w com sc int BRC

Don't put off being honest (McCoy) 1m 2w com sc int MOD

Door should be either open or shut (Musset) 2m sc French int BF

Door was closed (Arlett) 4m 2w Ic sc. so. American int WAR

Dope (Lee) 6m 3w ext sc int FR

J   Dorothea dances the minuet (Quinlan) 3b 4g sc int QU

Double date (Ryerson) 3m 4w com sc int FR

J n–r   Double 9 of Chih Yuan (Nolan) 5b 2g sc Chinese int NO

J n–r   Double talk (McCoy) 2b Ig com sc int MCO

c   Dragon who giggled (McCormick) 7 characters sc exterior FR

c   Dragon's tooth (Richardson) 4b 3g ext sc. open space RIC

Dreaming dust (Johnson) 10m 3w sc St. Patrick's cathedral JOH

J   Dr. Heidegger's experiment (Robinson) 4b Ig sc int BAK

J   Dr. in spite of himself (Moliere) 6b 3g sc French int OLI

Dr. Killemquick's medicine (Fisher) 2m Ib Ig ext com sc stage BRHM

c n–r   Dr. Time's office (Very) 5b 2g ext sc office VE

Druid's ring (Morris) 8w sc Druid's circle BAK
Dry river bed (Spark) 2m 6w sc African int SP

c   Dulce man (Blanton) 4b 2g sc small park in Mexico PLA
C   Dumb sentry (Smith) 3b sc sentry post SMI
Dust of the road (Goodman) 3m Iw sc int FR
Duchess of Dogwood Lane (Elam) 3w 1b com sc int LO
Dwarf trees (Motokiyo) 4m Iw sc in Japan AN

E

Early frost (Parkhurst) 5w sc int FR
Easy exit (Lindley) 6w sc atomic research BAK
Easy money (Proverman) 4m Iw Sc living rm MA3
c n–r   Echo of '76 (Hark) 4b Ig sc int HAR
Edge o'dark (John) 5m Iw sc mine in England JN
J   Edison's light (Reines) 9b ext sc laboratory REI
R   Education for death (Zeimer) Nar announcer 10m 6w orchestra
        BAC
R   Education for life (Atkinson) 10m 3w orchestra chorus BAC
Educating Josefina (Villa) 1m 2w com sc int in Philippines EDS
R   Education for victory (Atkins) Nar announcer 2m 2w 5c sc
        radio BAC
J   Eenie, meenie, minee, murder (Murray) 5b 5g sc int MUR
Efficient expert (Taylor) 5m 5w ext com sc office EDS
J   1804 (Somerscales) 12b 4g ext sc sea front SO
c n–r   Election day in the USA (Newman) 9b 3g ext sc polling place
        NEW
Eldest (The) (Ferber) 4m 3w sc dining rm COO
Elevator (Gardner) 5m Iw sc int FR
Eleventh hour (Anthony) 3m sc office WAR
c J   Eliezer Ben Yehudah (Citron) Nar 13b 6g voice sc stage CI
Elisha & the Long Knives (Wasserman) 6b Ig ext sc cabin KON
Eliza & the Lexicon (Greene) Im 2w sc beach MA5
Elizabeth Blackwell (Fox) 3m 5w Sc frontier int POG
Elopement (The) (Drummond) 5m 2w com sc R.R. station BRG
Embers (Beckett) 7m Iw ext voice sc sea BEC
J   Emergency doctor (Miksch) Ib Ig sc int MH
Emperor Jones (O'Neil) 10m Iw sc outdoors DO
c n–r   Emperor's new clothes (Newman) 6b 2g ext sc throne room
        NEW
J c   Emperor's nightingale (Anderson) 7b 5g sc garden PLA
Emperor's nightingale (Totheroh) 9m 3w ext com sc stage FR
Empty bowls (Fisher) 2 speakers, voices 9 characters sc stage
        FIU
c   Enchanted Christmas tree (Wilde) 2m Iw 19c sc int FR
End game (Beckett) 4m sc. int BEB BEK
End it all (McCoy) Im Iw com sc int MOD

J   **End of the line** (Miksch) 5b 2g voice sc football stadium MH

T   **End of the story** (Gilbert) 7m lw sc graveyard HAL

        End of the term (Barrow) 4m sc school BAK

        Engggarrdel! (Daumal) 12 characters sc field BEN

c   **Enter, George Washington** (Hark) 2b 3g sc int PLA

        Enter the hero (Helburn) 1m 3w com sc int FR

        Entertaining sister's beaux (George) 2m 2w com sc int BRHM

J   **Entertainment Com'n** (Miksch) 1b 4g com sc int MH

        Era of Vincent van Gogh (Bridie) 1m 1w sc studio BR

        Eternal life (Eastman) 2m 3w 1b sc air raid shelter FR

J   **Evacuation day** (Follen) any number of characters BAK

        Evening bells (Miksch) com sc int MH

        Evening star (George) 4m 6w com sc theatre BRI

        Ever on Christmas (Phillips) 5w sc stage POW

J   **Every room with bath** (Murray) 5b 6g com sc hotel lobby MU

        Everybody comes to Mabel (Morris) 7w com sc int EV

J n–r   **Everyday is Thanksgiving** (Du Bois) 4b 5g sc int BUW

        Everyman (———) Any number of characters, sc none BRT CLI HN

c   **Everywhere Christmas** (Very) 15b 9g ext sc int Ve

J   **Expanding trade** (Miksch) 4b 2g com sc porch MH

        Express for Santiago (Aguirre) 3m 2w ext sc R.R. station MA4

        Extremes meet (Housman) 3m 2w sc Westminister castle HO

        Eye-opener (An) (Drummond) 3m com sc street BRJ

        Eyes upon the cross (Mueller) Nar 11m 11w eb sc stage BAD

F

        Fabulous tale (Stockton) 7m 1w extras sc "skid row" MA2

R   **Face of America** (Wolfe) Announcer 1m 1w orchestra sc radio DAO

J   **Facing the future** (Hackett) 4m 2g com sc int BAK

c n–r   **Fairy circus** (Very) 4b 1g extras sc int VE

T   **Faith hawker** (Rodman) Nar 2m 2w sc stage GUN

        Faithless (The) (Hayden) 4m sc outdoors FR

        Falstaff at Gadshill (———) 6m extras sc London tavern HL

        Fall of man (York) 3m 1w sc garden BRT

R   **Fall of the city** (MacLeish) Announcer 6m 1w voices extras sc studio RED

        Family (The) (Casey) Nar 1m 1w 1b sc stage CAT

        Family album (Coward) 5m 4w com int COW

        Family tree (Price) 12w sc BAK

c J R   **Family under the bridge** (Carlson) 5b 2g voices sc int OK

J   **Famous families** (Emurian) 15b 4g extras sc int EMM

        Fanny, the farmer's daughter (Price) 3m 5w com sc int BRG

        Farce of the worthy Master Pierre Patelin (————) 4m 1w sc French int CL1

T	**Flight of the dove** (Wilson) 7m 3w sc airplane landing BAS
	Florentine tragedy (Wilde) 2m 1w sc. home in Italy CER
c n-r	**Flower garden** (Very) 23 characters sc garden VE
	Flowers & weeds (Drummond) 16 characters sc park BRJ
	Flowers for the dead (Flores) 2m 6w sc cemetery MON
	Fog (Neuenburg) 3w sc int BAK
	Fog (O'Neil) 3m 1w extras sc shipwreck ON
	Foiled again, or saved by fate (Drummond) 2m 2w com sc stage BRG
c	**Food for freedom** (Kauffman) 7b 4g sc int BAK
	For distinguished service (Knox) 3w sc int BAK
	For his brother's crime (Price) 4m 4w sc int BRG
c	**For soldiers everywhere** (Carlson) 1b 4g extras sc farmhouse CAR
	For the land's sake! (Drummond) Nar 3m 2w com sc int BRG
	For the time being (Auden) Any number of characters sc church HALI
	For want of a character (Quinn) 5m 4w com sc tavern LO
	For women only (McCoy) 12w com sc traffic intersection MCJ
J	**Forbidden Christmas** (Konick) 5b 2g extras sc City square KON
c n-r	**Forest fantasy** (Hark) 9b 6g extras sc forest HAR
	Forever Eve (Lothrop) 7g com sc int BAK
	Forever Judy (Lindsay) 2m 3w com sc int FR
c n-r	**Forgotten hero** (Miller) 5b 5g sc stage MIG
c	**Fortune of Merrylegs & tawny-whiskers** (Molloy) 9b sc old inn BUR
J	**Forty winks** (Somerscales) 1b 3g sc int SO
C n-r	**Forward march** (Hark) 4b 1g sc stage HAR
	Fountains of youth (Huber) 5m 2w com sc stage HU
	Four Chaplains (Citron) Nar 15 boys sc stage CI
J n-r	**Four in a tower** (Barboo) 7g com sc int BAK
	Four p.p. (——) 4m sc public rm HN
	Four Queens wait for Henry (Peach) 5w com sc next world BOU4
c	**Four wishes** (Kissen) 4b 2g sc int KIR
	Fourth for Bridge (Johnson) 7m sc Italian aircraft JOH
J	**Freddy the detective** (Brooks) 1b 1g OK
	Free samples (Huber) 3m 2w com sc int HU
c J	**Freedom hall** (Franklin) 4b 1g extras sc hall CI
R	**Freedom's a hard-bought thing** (Benet) Nar 5m 2w sc stage FQ
J n-r	**French cabinetmaker** (Nolan) 3b 5g sc shop NO PLA
	Fresco for Unesco (Fisher) 1b 1g extras sc in the U.N. FIU
J	**Fresh start for the Beales** (St Clair) 3b 3g sc int SAI
	Friday's Thursday off (McCoy) 2m com sc desert island MOD
	Fright (Reach) 3m 2w sc street FR
c	**Frog Prince** (Kissen) 4b 2g sc garden of the palace KIR
	From five to five-thirty (Johnson) 5w com sc int FR

c J   Giant of the timber (McCaslin) 14b lg story teller sc outside
      MCC
      Giant stair (Steele) 2m 2w sc mountain cabin FR
      Gift (Foley) 2m 1w sc house in Judea FR
c J n–r Gift of old St. Nick (Fisher) 3b 3g sc int FIR
c J   Gift of corn (McCaslin) 8b 5g sc Indian wigwam MCC
J   Gift of laughter (Dias) 4b 4g sc cabin DIA
      Gift of music (James) 2m 3w sc int BRH
c   Gift of the Holy Spirit (Phillips) 6b voices sc anywhere PHI
c n–r Gift to the world (Newman) 19 characters sc in a German town
      NEW
      Gift twice given (Wefer) 4w sc int BAK
c n–r Gifts of the New Year (Miller) 3b 16g sc throne rm MIE
c n–r Gifts for young Abe (Very) 1b 1g ext sc log cabin VE
n–r   Gifts of St Patrick (McMullen) sc church assembly FR
R   Gigolo & gigolette (Maugham) 18m 6w Nar sc radio MAU
      Gin & bitterness (Richards) 4m 4w sc apartment MA3
c R   Ginger Pye (Estes) 3b 2g sc int OK
      Girdle around the earth (Lowe) 4w sc int BAK
      Give us this day (Guder) 3w sc ancient Palestine GUD
      Glamour (Wilde) 2m 2w sc theatre WH
      Glass menagerie (Williams) 2m 2w sc alley in St. Louis HAV
      WE
c n–r Glass slippers (Miller) 7b 5g sc workshop MIE
      'Gloria mundi (Brown) 2m 4w sc insane asylum FR
c n–r Glory he deserves (Hark) 12b 3g sc platform HAR
      Glory in the flower (Inge) 5m 1w sc roadhouse CER
      Go down Moses (Lamb) 3m ext voices sc stage BAD
      Go, ye faithful witnesses (Miller) any number of characters sc
      church MIZ
      God's available power (Miller) Nar choir 4m 4w sc stage MIZ
c   Going home from the dance (Smith) 1b 1g sc street SMI
c J   Going to a party (Podolyn) 1b 1g sc street CI
c   Gold for my cakes (Kissen) 3b 4g sc street KIR
c   Gold in your garden (Asbrand) 3b 4g sc garden PLA
T   Goldbergs (Berg) 4m 3w com sc television SET
c   Goldilocks & the three bears (Pratt) 2b 2g puppet sc stage PR
      Golden axe (Scholl) 2m 1w sc farmhouse in the Ozarks MA2
c n–r Golden bell for mother (Very) 14 characters sc int VE
c   Golden goose (Kissen) 4b 5g sc woods KIR
J   Golden goose (Sloane) 5b 2g ext sc outdoors SL
      Golden hearts (Slattery) 6b 5g sc throne rm PLA
R J   Golden touch (Longstreth) Nar 6b sc California gold rush POO
j n–r Golden voice of little Erik (Nolan) 6b 3g sc street NO
      Gone tomorrow (Harrity) 5m 2w com sc int in Ireland DRA
      Good & the evil (Casey) Nar soloist chorus 3m 1w sc platform
      CAT

c **Good ghosts** (Hosking) 6c sc screens JA

  Good night Caroline (Seiler) 2m 2w com sc int DRA

  Good woman of Setzuan (Brecht) large number of characters sc
   city gate in China REH

  Goodbye, my gentle (Nolledo) 6m 1w sc int in Philippines FL

  Goodbye to the clown (Kinoy) 3m 3w sc circus com FR

  Goodbye to the Lazy K (Finch) 5m 1w sc ranch house ZA

  Goodnight please (Daggett) 4m 3w sc int FR

  Gospel witch (Phelps) 8m 4w ext sc in early Salem HAL3

  Gossip shop (Wilde) 8w com sc int BAK

  Governor (The) (Barling) 9m 1w sc in India WAR

  Grab & grace (Williams) 5m 1w sc int HAL3 WIL

J **Graduation present** (Orme) 8b 1g sc newspaper office KAM

  Grandma (Howe) 3m 2w sc farmhouse BRI

J **Grandpa & the statue** (Miller) announcer 10b sc Army hospital
   POG

c **Granny Goodman's Christmas** (Bennett) 7b 5g sc kitchen KAN

  Granny's rose (Sando) 5m 2w 5c sc garden SAN

J n–r **Gray flannel blues** (Murray) 6m 6w com sc int MUC

c J **Great charoses** (Segal) 7 roles 1 voice sc meeting rm SEF SEG

  Great choice (Eastman) 4m 4w sc int FR

  Great highways (Strindberg) 15m 5w sc road SP

c **Great Quillow** (Smith) 14b sc village square SM

c J **Great women of Israel** (Aronin) Nar 21 characters sc stage CI

  Greatest gift (Lord) 4m 3w 4c sc int FR

c n–r **Greedy goblin** (Miller) 6b 3g sc int MIG

c **Greek merchant & the lions** (Smith) Nar 7b sc ancient Rome
   SMI

  Green room blues (Carmichael) 7w com sc womans club BAK

  Greene Christmas (A) (Preston) 8m 8w com sc int BRH

J n–r **Greetings from the Fultons** (McCoy) 3b 3g com sc int MCO

c **Greta & the Princess** (Cooper) 2b 3g Nar sc cottage DUR

  Guardian (O'Brien) 3m 4w sc in ancient Palestine FR

n–r **Guest house, very exclusive** (Edmonds) 4m 6w sc int FR

J **Gulliver wins his freedom** (Howard) 12b 2g ext sc seashore
   HOW

c **Gypsy's finger ring** (Richardson) 1b 4g sc outdoors RIC

H

  Half an hour (Barrie) 3m 2w sc int BAR

c **Half-pint cowboy** (Miller) 23b sc Bar X ranch MIF

T **Hall of Ivy** (Colman) 5m 1w com sc television SET

J n–r **Halloween luck** (Hark) 3b 3g sc int HAT

c **Ham actor** (Smith) 2b sc street SMI

  Ham that am (The) (Sheldon) announcer 3b 3g sc stage BRJ

  Hand maid of God (Sando) 4w sc rm in ancient Damascus SAN

J T	Hand-me-down (Cotton) 4m 3w com sc int DEC
	Hands across the sea (Coward) 5m 3w sc drawing rm com CER **COW**
J R	Hands across the sea (Schneideman) announcer 7b 2g sc int SCH
c	Handy man (Smith) 1b 1g int SMI
	Hangs over thy head (Purkey) 3m 2w sc stage MAI
c	Hansel & Gretel (Simonds) Nar 2b 1g sc cottage DUR
n-r	Happy ending of a gruesome ghost (Relonde) 4m 2w 1g eb sc int JA
c n-r	Happy holidays (Newman) 21 characters sc workshop NEW
J	Happy holidays for Little Women (Howard) Nar 5b 4g sc parlor HOW
	Happy journey to Camden & Trenton (Wilder) 3m 3w sc journey FR CARS CER COO
	Happy pagan (Ouzts) 1m 1w sc woodland LO
J n-r	Happy Valentine's day (Garver) 3b 2g sc int BUW
J	Harmony a la hobo (Drummond) 4b com sc outdoors BRJ
	Harrowing of hell (York) 7m sc church BRT
	Hat (Provence) 2w hat store BRC
J n-r	Hats & rabbits (Pendleton) sc int BUW
J	Haunted clothesline (Miller) 11b 5g sc back yard PLA
J n-r	Haunts for hire (Miller) 8b 6g sc office MIL
	Have a good time (Steele) any number of characters com sc int BRHM
	Haym Salomon (Bach) 7m 1w sc office BAK
J	Haym Solomon's battle (Fisher) 9b 5g sc office FIS
	He is risen (Miller) 2 solo groups extras sc church MIZ
c J	He traveled the world (McCaslin) 4b 1g story teller sc farmhouse MCC
n-r	Headless horseman (Hunterton) 7m 2w 2b sc int JA
c J	Healing at the pool of Bethesda (Phillips) 5b int extras PHI
c J	Healing of the man born blind (Phillips) 5b sc in the Temple PHI
c J	Healing of the paralyzed man (Phillips) 5b 2g sc outside house PHI
J n-r	Heart trouble (Hark) 3b 2g sc int HAT
	Heat lightning (Carroll) 2m 1w bus com FR
	Heathen pioneer (Climenhagan) 2m 2w sc int FR
	Heaven is a long time wait (Conkle) 2 adults 2c sc farm MA3
	Heavenly robe of feathers (Motokiyo) 3m ext sc river AN
	Heavy change (Housman) 4m 2w sc palace HO
c	Heavy chiffonier (Smith) sc stairs SMI
c	Heidi (Freeman) 13 characters sc mountain side FR
	Hello out there (Saroyan) 3m 2w FR MOO
	Help wanted (Nalasco) 3m 3w com sc int EDS
J	Help wanted—badly (Miksch) 3b 2g com sc int MH

Helping hand (Miksch) 2b 2g com sc dining rm MH
Henry, the model husband (Drummond) 1m 2w com sc int BRJ
Henry, the model husband (Phelps) 1m 2w com sc int BRHM
Her affairs in order (Bolton) 6w sc bed rm EV
Her Christmas hat (Hare) 4m 5w sc int BRH
Her majesty comes home (Singsbee) Nar 5w sc int BRC
Herbert's hurt (Huber) 3w com sc int BRC
Here we are (Parker) 2m 2w sc compartment in Pullman CER
Herod & the Kings (Coventry) sm medieval church BRT

J R Herod & the Magi (Malcolmson) Announcer 7b 2g ext sc church MAL

c Heroine of Wren (Colbo) Nar 4b 2g sc cottage DUR

c J Herzl comes home (Citron) 19 characters sc stage CI

Hewers of coal (Corrie) 5m sc coal mine BAK

J Hiding place (Quinlan) 2b 4g sc colonial home QU

R High flight (Magee) Announcer 6m 3w orchestra sc stage BAC

High pressure (McCoy) 2m 3w com sc int MCJ
High pressure (Drummond) 2m 1w com sc int BRJ
High school (Perl) 7m 3w sc int MAI

J n-r Highland fling (Nolan) 4b 4g sc open country NO

Highland lad (Very) 3m 2w sc kitchen JA

c J Hillel the student (Segal) 5b sc academy in ancient Israel CI

J n-r His & hers (Murray) 3m 4w com sc int MU

J His first date (Reach) 2b 4g com sc int FR

R His honor, the mayor (Welles) 4m 2w sc radio FQ

His sister (Provence) 2w sc hospital BRC

Historical hystericals (Kaser) 6m 6w com sc outdoors BRHM

J Hitch-hiker (Fletcher) 8b 4g sc auto camp KON

J n-r Hold back the redskins (Dias) 10b 3g sc outdoors DIA

Hold onto your hat (Richter) 8w com sc hat shop POX

J n-r Hold your hat (McCoy) 2b 4g com sc millinery store MCO

c n-r Holiday for Santa (Nicholson) 8b 1g sc shop KAN

J Holiday homecoming (Miksch) 4b 4g com sc int MH

c J Holiday minstrels (Zweig) 4b singers sc curtains CI

Hollywood fever (Winthrop) 6w sc int BAK

J Hollywood horseplay (Miksch) 9b 6g com sc motion picture studio MH

Holy experiment (Sando) 2m 2w sc woods SAN

J Home in the country (Murray) 4b 6g com farmhouse MUR

Home life of buffalo (Harrity) 3m 2w com sc int DRA

c Home, sweet home (Werner) 7b sc barnyard BUR

J n-r Homecoming (Hark) 2b 4g sc int HAT

J Honest Abe Lincoln (Fisher) 4b 4g sc log cabin FIS

J R Honest Injun! (Murray) 8b 2g com sc int MU

J Honored one (Leuser) 8b 4g sc rm in palace PLA

J Honoring friendship (Ritari) 2b 5g ext sc int in Pan America BAK

I'll take you home again Kathleen (Emurian) Nar 4m 1w sc ship EMM

I'm not here (Huber) 1m 5w com sc int HU

J   Imaginary trial of George Washington (Wolman) 15b 3g sc court BUW

J R   Immigrants all, Americans all (Fisher) Nar 11b 7g sc stage FIS

Impromptu (Mosel) 2m 2w sc stage DRA

In Abraham's bosom (Green) 10m 2w sc woods GR

J   In dulci jubilo (Somerscales) 1b 1g ext sc church SO

c n–r In honor of trees (Newman) 11 characters ext sc woods NEW

c   In the days of King Alfred (Holmes) Nar 2b 1g sc in ancient England DUR

In the land of schmozz (Sheldon) Nar 3b 1g sc stage BRJ

In the nick of time (Drummond) 3m 1w com sc stage BRG

In the Rector's study (John) 4m 6w sc int JN

In the shadow of the glen (Synge) 3m 1w sc Irish cottage CER

In the valley (Green) 8m 2w sc int in the South FR

In the zone (O'Neil) 9m sc seamen's forecastle ON

In union (Huber) 5w com sc int BRC HU

J   Inasmuch (Emurian) 5b 1g ext soloist sc int EMM

Inca of Jerusalem (Shaw) 1m 1w sc hotel SHA

Incident at Standish Arms (Inge) 1m 3w sc living rm IN

Income tax (Lynch) 3m 2w com sc int FR

Inconsequential journeys (Sheldon) announcer any number of characters sc stage BRJ

n–r   Indignant ghost (Dustmann) 2m 2w 7c sc int JA

Infanta (Olfson) 2m 3w sc int in Spain POX

c J n–r Inn at Bethlehem (Fisher) 11b 5g ext sc stage CJ

Innocence triumphs (Donald) 3m 1w com sc int BRG

Innocent bystander (Huber) 2m 1w com sc street corner HU

J R   Inside a kid's head (Lawrence) Announcer 12 characters sc radio KON

J n–r Instructions for Gary (McCoy) 2b 3g com sc int MCO

Interlude (Carroll) 3m 1w sc market town CARR

Intermezzo (Godefroy) 3w sc dressing rm in opera EV

"Interruptions, interruptions" (Ludwig) 2b 1g sc express train CARV

Interview (The) (Spark) 1m 2w sc flat SP

c   Invasion of the stratosphere (Fisher) Nar 5b 2g sc planet DUR JIU

J   Invisible inventions, inc. (Murray) 7b 2g com sc office MUC

Invisible Key (Neuenburg) 5w sc int BA

J n–r Invisible man (Wells) Nar 7b 4g sc stormy night OLI

J   Is thrift a virtue? (Miksch) 2b 1g com sc bank MH

It happened in Irkutsk (Arbuzov) 19 characters ext sc Russian int WE

It happened on Kol Nidre night (Segal) 14 roles sc Israel SEF SEG

It might happen (George) announcer 4m com sc end of the world BRHM

It should happen to a dog (Mankowitz) 2m com sc sea FR HAL3

J   Italian love song (Murray) 5b 5g com sc int MUR

It's a silly game (Huber) 1m 3w com sc basketball game BRJ

c   It's Christmas again (Asbrand) 7b 7g sc int BAK

It's her or the car (Steele) 3m 1w sc int BRHM

J   It's no picnic (Miksch) 4b 3g com sc garden MH

c   It's tough on mother (Casey) 2b 2g sc int CAS

J

J Caesar (Harris) 10m sc int BAK

c n–r   Jack & the beanstalk (Very) 5b 4g ext sc garden VE

T   Jack Benny program (Benny) 4m 1w com sc television SET

T   Jack Paar show (Paar) 4m com sc television

Jacob comes home (Kozlenko) 2m 3w sc in Hitler's Germany ZA

c   Jane Addams (Kissen) 4b 6g ext sc Hull house KIS

R   Jarvis bay (Fowler) Nar announcer orchestra 2m sc radio BAC

J   Jeanne D'Arc (Grimes) 1b 5g sc in medieval France BAK

c J   Jerusalem (Citron) Nar 22 characters ext sc stage CI

Jest of Hahalaba (Dunsany) 4m sc house in London CER

c   Jesus appears in Galilee (Phillips) 5b sc sea PHI

c   Jesus appears to his disciples (Phillips) 6b voices sc tomb PHI

c   Jesus returns to Galilee (Phillips) 4b lakeside PHI

Jet of blood (Artaud) 7m 3w sc int BEN

c   Jim Bridger & his eight-hour echo (Carlson) 2b 1g sc plains CAR

c   Jiminy cinders (Miller) 8b sc bunkhouse BUR

J   Jimmy & the same old stuff (Martens) 2b 4g ext sc int BAK

J n–r   Jimmy six (Downing) 2b 3g sc int BUU PLA

Jinxed (Mosel) 4m 1w sc lunch rm CART FR

J   Jobs for girls (Bollans) 8g com sc int BAK

Joey (Else) 5m 3w sc stage MA5

Johan, Johan (————) 4m 1w sc int HN

J   John Crowe's legacy (Suerken) 25b sc stage BUR

c n–r   John Grumlie (Very) 5b 4g sc farmhouse VE

c J R   John Henry (McCaslin) 2 story tellers 9b 2g sc railroad MCC

J   John Jewitt (Emmons) 5b 1g sc outdoors EM

John Shanahan, me boy (Casey) 6 characters com sc orphanage FR

c   Johnny Aladdin (Wallerstein) 8b 5g ext sc saloon WAL

J n–r   Johnny Appleseed (Nolan) 6b 3g sc woods NO

J   Johnny Appleseed in danger (Howard) Nar 12 characters ext sc woods HOW

K

c   **Kitten capers** (Boiko) any number of characters sc classroom
         PLA
         Kitty Hawk—1903 (Ickler) Nar 5b 1g sc field DUR
         Knight before Christmas (Preston) 8m 8w sc R R station BRH
c n–r   **Knight of safety** (Hark) 10b 4g sc woodland HAR
J n–r   **Know the truth** (Hark) 3b 1g sc int BUW
         Krapp's last tape (Beckett) 1m 1w sc den BEC
         Kupid's college (McCoy) 1m 1w ext com sc campus MOD

L

c n–r   **Lacey's last garland** (Miller) 2b 5g sc int MIG
         Ladies in jeopardy (Bennett) 7w sc England of Henry VIII BAK
         Ladies-in-waiting (Maule) 7w sc hospital EV
c J   **Lady Esther from Shushaiyen** (Segal) announcer 12 roles sc
         office SEF SEG
         Lady Precious Stream (Hsiung) reader 4m 3w ext sc curtains
         RED
         Land of heart's desire (Yeats) 3m 3w poetic sc. Irish cottage FR
         Landing of Columbus (Kaser) 6m ext com sc sea landing BRHM
j n–r   **Landslide for Shakespeare** (Dias) 8b 8g com sc drug store DIA
         Last horizon (McCaslin) 5m 6w sc rm in Boston MCB
         Last judgment (York) 6m ext sc medieval church BRT
         Last of the Lowries (Green) 1m 3w sc rural FR
c   **Last supper** (Phillips) 5b voices sc int PHI
         Last war (Grant) 9 characters sc open places WAR
         Last word (Broughton) 1m 1w sc a bar HAL3
         Lavender kite (Seidelhuber) 2m 1w sc int FR
         Lawyer Lincoln (Smith) 4m 5w sc boarding house POX
T J   **Lawyer Lincoln** (Webb) 4b 5g sc court house BAK
         Lay this body down (Green) 2m 1w 3c sc int FR
         Leading Lady (McCaslin) story teller 5m 6w sc stage MCB
J n–r   **Leak in the dike** (Nolan) 4b 4g sc dike NO
         Leak in the Universe (Richards) 4m 1w voices sc institute NEV
J R n–r **Left-over reindeer** (Miller) 9 characters sc radio KAN
J   **Legend beautiful** (St. Clair) Reader 3b sc church SAI
         Legend of Minnie Lamourrie (McCaslin) story teller 4m 4w
         ext sc woods MCB
c n–r   **Legend of the Christmas rose** (Leuser) 7b 3g ext sc road KAN
         Lemon curd (Beeche) 6w sc int BAK
         Lens maker (Gilmore) 5b 1g ext sc workshop POO
         Leprechaun (The) (Purkey) 3m 1w sc shoemaker's hut POX
J R   **Lesson (The)** (Harrison) 1b 3g ext sc mining town KON
         Lesson (The) (Ionesco) 1m 2w com sc int FR REI
R   **Lesson in Japanese** (Hopkins) Nar 2m 2w orchestra chorus sc
         radio BAC

Let freedom ring (Miller) 4m ext sc int MIZ

c n–r   Let George do it (Hark) 3b 3g sc int HAR

Let go the dream (Purkey) 5m 3w sc stable MA5

Let man live (Lagerkvist) 10m 3w sc stage HAL3

Let there be bread (Fisher) 15m 9w sc int FIU

Let there be farce (Walsh) 1m 2w sc in the slums MAI

Let's get out of here (Welsh) announcer 2m 1w sc shabby
        hotel rm MA2

Let's modernize (Huber) 5w com sc int BRJ

Let's pretend (Huber) 2m 2w com sc int HU

R   Letter from a Red army man (Grabotov) announcer 1m 1w sc
        stage BAC

J   Letter to Sam (Murray) 4b 3g com sc lobby of hotel MUR

Liar's club (Stahl) chairman 5m com sc int BRHM

c   Library circus (Miller) 9b ext sc library MIF

J n–r   Licha's birthday serenade (Nolan) 6b 8g sc yard NO

J   Life for mother (Hark) 3b 3g sc int PLA

Life in the Highlands (Housman) 1m 2w 2c sc outdoors HO

J   Life is so dull (Miksch) 3b 2g com sc int MH

T   Life of Riley (Bendix) announcer 3m 2w sc television SET

n–r   Light on Beacon Hill (Miller) 2m 2w ext sc int FR

Light on Slane (Phillips) 4m ext sc int BAK

c R   Light on Tern rock (Sauer) 3b 3g sc light house OK

J   Light within (St. Clair) 3b 3g sc int SAI

J n–r   Like mother used to make (Murray) 5b 5g com sc kitchen MUC

Lincoln reckons up (Stevens) 5m ext sc int BAK

c n–r   Lincoln's library fine (Miller) 5b 5g sc int MIE

c   Lion & the mouse (Barr) 5b sc int DUR

c   Little bear tries to see Santa Claus (Pratt) 4b 2g puppet sc
        stage PR

c J   Little candle that wouldn't (Hyman) Nar 15 characters sc int CI

c n–r   Little Chip's Christmas tree (Duvall) 19b 9g ext sc int KAN

c n–r   Little fir tree (Very) 6b 2g sc outside VE

c n–r   Little friends (Very) 11 characters sc forest VE

Little learning (A) (Brosius) 4w sc int FR

J   Little lost leprechaun (Martens) any number of characters sc
        outdoors BAK

J n–r   Little man who wasn't there (Dias) 2m 5w com sc int DIA

c n–r   Little nut tree (Miller) 10b 7g sc garden MIE

Little poor man (Copeau) 27m 2w sc stage HAY

c   Little Princess (Burnett) 3b 9g sc attic rm PLA

c   Little Princess (Brown) Commentator 1b 9g sc int BRO

n–r   Little prison (Savage) 5w sc stalled elevator BAK

c   Little red hen (Tichenor) 3b 1g puppet sc stage TI

c   Little red hen & the grain of wheat (Sloane) 4b 1g ext chorus
        sc outside SL

c   Little Red Riding Hood (McCrae) 2b 3g puppets sc int MCR

c   **Little Red Riding Hood** (Sheldon) Nar 3g sc stage BRJ
J n–r **Little women** (Alcott) Nar 7g 1b sc int OLI
c   **Little women** (Brown) Commentator 6g sc int BRO
n–r   **Little women** (Morley) 8g int KAN
c   **Littlest month** (Faux) Nar 9b 4g sc int DUR
c   **Littlest shepherd** (Ryerson) 9b 3g sc outdoors FR
       Living dead man (Rojo) 4m com sc forest EDS
J   **Living dramatization of the beatitudes** (Emurian) Nar 13b sc
           stage EMM
R n–r **Lock, stock & barrel** (Murray) 6b 6g com sc theatre MU
c R   **Lone hunt** (Steele) 4b 1g sc outdoors OK
R   **Lonesome train** (Lampell) Nar any number of characters sc
           exterior COO
c n–r **Long ago in Bethlehem** (Newman) 1b 5g ext sc inn yard NEW
       Long Christmas dinner (Wilder) 5m 7w sc int FR
       Long journey home (O'Neil) 6m 2w ext sc waterfront dive
           DRA UL
J   **Long may it wave** (Fisher) 2b 2g sc int FIS
       Long shot (Massey) 9w sc club BAK
       Long view (Arthur) 5m 3w com sc university FR
C   **Lord's prayer** (Phillips) 5b sc desert PHI
       Lord's will (Green) 1m 2w sc int FR
J   **Lost birds** (Somerscales) 3b 1g sc int SO
       Lost Christmas (Kimes) 4m 3w sc int FR
c   **Lost Christmas card** (Miller) 7b 6g sc street corner MIF
c   **Lost Princess** (Totheroh) 12 characters ext sc chinese screens FR
       Louis Pasteur (Reines) 16b 4w sc int REI
       Love (Miller) 4m 4w sc church MIZ
       Love errant (Narl) 2m 2w com sc int FR
       Love knoweth no bounds (Drummond) 3m 1w reader com sc
           outside BRG
c   **Love that tractor** (Smith) 7b 1g sc in Russia SMI
J R   **Love your neighbor** (Schneideman) Announcer 8b sc radio SCH
       Loving—giving (Sando) 2b 1g ext sc altar SAN
J   **Love's in fashion** (Murray) 7b 7g sc fashion salon PLA MUC
       Love's labor (Huber) 3m 2w com sc int HU
       Lowly milkman (Kaser) 3m 4w com sc lawn BRG
c   **Lucky piece for Mom** (Casey) 3b 3g sc int CAS
J n–r **Luncheon for three** (McCoy) 2b 3g com sc int MCO

M

R   **Mad islands** (Macneice) 9m 5w sc ancient Ireland MA
c   **Mad tea party** (Worcester) Nar 3b 1g sc int DUR
       Madame Curie (Osborn) 3m 1w sc classrm in Paris BE DEC
n–r   **Madame Dode** (West) 2m 5w sc int JA
J   **Madison Ave. merry-go-round** (Dias) 4b 5g sc office DIA

J	Magic Box (Moore) 7m 4w sc throne rm PLA
c n–r	Magic carpet sweeper (Miller) 3b 3g sc int MIG
c n–r	Magic egg (Hark) 8b 9g sc forest HAR
c	Magic fishbone (Barnes) 4b 4g sc int FEN
c	Magic fishbone (Smith) 2b 3g ext sc int SM
c	Magic goose (Newman) Nar 12b 5g sc fair grounds DUR
c n–r	Magic goose (Newman) announcer 7b 4g sc fair grounds NEW
J n–r	Magic of Salamanca (Nolan) 4b 2g sc road NO
c	Magic pencils (Miller) 9b 7g sc garden of learning PLA
c J	Magic top (Solis—Cohn) 11 characters sc stage CI
c	Magic well (Leuser) 12b 7g sc wishing well PLA
c J	Magician (Citron) 4b 3g sc home in Poland CI
C	Mail order dragon (Stahl) Nar 3b 1g com sc in China BRJ
T	Make room for Daddy (Thomas) 4m 1w com sc television SET
	Maker of dreams (Down) 2m 1w sc curtains FR CER
c	Making mother over (Casey) 4g sc int CAS
J	Making of Mark Twain (Reines) 6b 3g sc int REI
	Male, model (Huber) 1m 3w com sc int HU
	Mall (The) (Inge) 3m 4w sc amusement park IN
J	Man behind the book (Phillips) 4b 4g sc library BUW
	Man in the bowler hat (Milne) 4m 2w com sc int FR
J n–r	Man like Lincoln (Miller) 5b 4g sc office MIL
	Man of destiny (Shaw) 3m 1w voice sc restaurant SH FE
c	Man of magic (Richardson) 6b 3g sc int RIC
	Man of many miens (Huber) 2m 1w com sc ticket office BRJ
	Man versus dog (Kaser) 3m com sc court rm BRHM
	Man who died at 12 o'clock (Green) 2m 1w com sc int FR
J	Man who lived too soon (Wilson) 9b 5g ext sc curtains BAK
	Man with the flower in his mouth (Pirandello) 2m sc int MOO
	Man with the question (Guder) Nar 2m 2w sc in Jerusalem GUD
J n–r	Mantle (The) (Dias) 9b 4g sc school office DIA
	Marriage proposal (Chekhov) 2m 1w com sc house in Russia CER
	Martha & Mary (Box) 7m 7w sc in Palestine FR
T	Martha Raye show (Raye) 5m 3w ext com sc television SET
	Mary Anne's mortgage (McCoy) 2m 2w com sc int MOD
c n–r	Mary's invitation (Miller) 3b 6g sc park MIG
J n–r	Master of the strait (Waite) 4b 3g sc kitchen KAN
J	May the best man win (Fisher) 3b 3g sc int FIS
C	May witch (Brydon) 8g sc play rm PLA
c	May day for mother (Miller) 10b 10g sc May day MIF
c n–r	Mayflower (Very) 18g ext sc yard VE
	Medicine man (Hyber) 2m 3w com sc stage HU
c n–r	Meet Mr. Muffin (Miller) 10b 9g sc int MIE
	Meeting in the town hall (Tan) 8m ext sc town hall EDS
	Meeting to music (Donovan) 10w ext musical sc stage BRC

c n–r Melody for Lincoln (Miller) 2b 6g sc int MIG
J R Melody man (Harmon) 9m 1w sc radio FEI
J R Melting pot (Schneideman) 9m 2g ext sc int SCH
c n–r Memorial Day for the blue & the gray (Newman) 3b 7g sc
        lawn NEW
      Memory course (McCoy) 1m 1w com sc office MOD
      Memory of summer (Inge) 1m 2w sc beach IN
      Memory of two Mondays (Miller) 12m 2w sc rm in warehouse
        CER MOO
      Memory saving time (Preston) 4w sc int BRC
      Mental marvel (Stahl) announcer 3m com sc curtains BRHM
      Mercy in moccasins (McCaslin) 5m 1w ext dancers sc forest
        MCB
      Mermaid avenue is the world (Goldman) 3m 4w boarding house
        MA4
J n–r Merry Christmas, Crawfords! (Hark) 6b 7g ext sc int KAN
c n–r Merry Christmas customs (Hark) 8b 2g ext sc int KAN
c   Merry Christmas elf (Fisher) 7b 5g ext sc stage FEN
      Merry Christmas in the old home town (Preston) any number
        of actors BRII
      Merry Mollie Malone (McCarthy) 3m 4w sc int in Ireland FR
c   Merry Tyll (Jagendorf) 9b 4g ext sc a market FEN
c n–r Merry-go-round for mother (Miller) 4b 11g sc curtains MIE
J   Midge rings the bell (Paradis) 10g sc dormitory KAM
      Midsummer night's play (Shakespeare) 4b 3g sc stage POG
      Mills that grind (Huber) 2m 2w sc doctor's waiting rm BRJ
      Mind of a killer (Kirkpatrick) 3m 2w sc inn FR
J n–r Mind over matter (Nicholson) 14b 4g sc general store BUU
c   Mind your P's & Q's (Hark) any number of actors sc stage PLA
      Mind's construction (McLaughlin) 5w university dormitory LO
      Minnie Fields (Conkle) 5m sc farm FR
J n–r Minority of millions (Hark) 11b 18g sc curtains BUU
J   Minstrels (The) (Somerscales) 4b 5g sc medieval hall SO
      Minuet (Parker) 2m 1w sc guillotine FR
      Miracle & the boar (Weber) 6m 2w sc rural scene in Ireland
        MA5
      Miracle for Mary (Burdin) 4m 9w sc outside cathedral FR
      Miracle in the Christmas city (McCaslin) 3m 2w sc fire place
        MCB
R   Miracle of the Danube (Anderson) 3m sc int FQ
c n–r Miraculous tea party (Miller) 7b 8g sc lawn MIG
      Mir-I-Nisa (Sicon) 5m voice sc int EDS
      Mirror—wardrobe one fine morning (Aragon) 5m 4w sc curtains
        BEN
J R n–r Mish—Mosh bird (Murray) 7b 5g ext com sc int MU
J   Miss Fix-it (McCoy) 3b 4g com sc int MCO

J   Miss Hepplewhite & the General (Murray) 4b 4g com sc rm
           MUR
J R   Miss Hepplewhite takes over (Murray) 4b 4g com sc office MU
J   Miss Herkimer's missile (Murray) 6b 3g com sc farmhouse MUR
           Miss Julie (Strindberg) 1m 2w sc kitchen MOO WE
R   Miss Liberty goes to town (Rosten) announcer 1m 6w orchestra
           BAC
c   Miss Muffet's wish (St. Clair) Nar 2b 2g sc lawn DUR
           Miss Tarzan into space (English) 8w com sc stage BOU7
           Missing false teeth (Sheldon) Reader 2m 1w com sc int BRJ
J n–r   Mister Twister (Murray) 5b 4g com sc int MUC PLA
J n–r   Mistletoe mystery (Miller) 5b 4g sc int MIL
           Mistress Minx (Haynes) 3w sc outdoors BAK
c J   Modern Modin (Kessler) 13g sc curtains CI
R   Modern Scrooge (Ruscoll) Nar announcer 8m sc stage BAC
R   Mole on Lincoln's cheek (Connelly) announcer 5m 1w sc school
           rm FQ
J   "Mollie Pitcher" (Fisher) 3b 1g sc orchard FIS
J n–r   Mom's perfect day (Hark) 5b 4g sc int HAT
           Money talks (Miller) any number of characters sc in darkest
           Africa MIZ
           Monkey's paw (Jacobs) 4m 1w sc int FR POE
J n–r   Monsieur Santa Claus (Miller) 9b 7g sc int KAN
           Monster (The) (Carson) 4w 8m sc rm in old house MA5
           Moon of the Caribbees (O'Neil) 15m 4w sc tramp steamer CER
           Moon shines on Kylenamoe (O'Casey) 6m 1w 1b 1g com sc
           village OC
           Moon up (Arthur) 3m 1w sc hills FR
J   Moon's up there (Nolan) 6b 4g sc rocket site PLA
c   Most memorable voyage (Bakeless) 10b ext voices sc deck of
           ship BUR
J n–r   Mother beats the band (Miller) 5b 10g sc int MIL
c   Mother earth's new dress (Hark) 5b 11g sc palace HAR
c   Mother Goose bakeshop (Miller) 8b 6g ext bakeshop MIF
c   Mother Goose's magic cookies (Blaine) 3b 5g sc kitchen PLA
J   Mother Goose's party (Fisher) 4b 6g sc int FIR
c   Mother hen (McCrea) Announcer 5 characters ext puppets sc
           stage MCR
           Mother remembers (Huber) 3w sc family rm BRC
c   Mothering Miss Mittie (Casey) 6b 7g sc int CAS
c n–r   Mother's admirers (Hark) 3b 3g sc int HAR
c n–r   Mother's fairy godmother (Miller) 2b 4g sc int MIG
J n–r   Mother's hidden talent (Miller) 8b 3g sc int BUW
           Mother's pet (Chalmers) 2w sc school rm BRC
J n–r   Mother's V I P's (Hark) 5b 4g sc int HAT
c n–r   Mouse that soared (Miller) 5b 1g sc meadow MIE

Movie man (O'Neil) 5m 1w sc house in Mexico ON
Moving finger (Wilde) 7m ext sc mythical country WH
J R n–r Mr. Filbert's claim to fame (Murray) 9b 5g ext sc hotel lobby
MU
Mr. Flannery's ocean (Carlino) 2m 4w 1b 1g sc int DRA
c n–r   Mr. Lincoln's beard (Newman) 5b 4g sc R R station NEW
J   Mr. Mumbly's miracle (Murray) 6b 4g com boarding house MUR
c J   Mr. Poppers penguins (Atwater) 4b 3g sc int OK
c J   Mr. Poppers penguins (Wright) Nar 8b 4g com sc street FEN
c J n–r Mr. Scrooge finds Christmas (Fisher) 14b 4g sc int FIS
c n–r   Mr. Snow White's Thanksgiving (Miller) 3b 4g sc farmhouse
MIG
Mrs. Bates at the P T A (Preston) 2w sc auditorium in school
BRC
Mrs. Charlie Chan (Haney) 8w sc lobby of hotel BRC
c n–r   Mrs. Claus' Christmas present (Urban) 5b 1g sc int KAN
J   Mrs. Harper's bazaar (Hughes) 8w com sc bazaar DRA
R   Mrs. Murgatroyd's dime (Latouche) 2m orchestra chorus sc
stage BAC
Mrs. Murphy's chowder (O'Hara) 2m 6w com sc int BAK
Mrs. O'Leary's cow (McCarthy) 2m 5w com sc barn FR
T   Mrs. Wickens in the fall (Kneale) 15m 5w sc int BAS
J   Mulcaster market (Reeves) 4b sc crossroads REE
c   Mummy's secret (McCrae) Nar 2b 4g puppet sc int MCR
Musical answers (Sheldon) announcer any number of characters
sc stage BRJ
Music cure (Shaw) 3m 1w sc drawing rm SHA
c J R   My cousin Avigdor (Wishengrad) Nar 7b sc settlement CI
J   My fair Linda (Carver) 4b 3g sc int PLA
J n–r   My host—the ghost (Murray) 4b 3g com sc int MUC
c n–r   Mystery at Knob Creek farm (Miller) 6b 5g sc grove MIG
Mystery manor (O'Brien) 8w sc int BRC
c n–r   Mystery of turkey—lurkey (Miller) 4b 2g sc barnyard MIG

N

J n–r   N for nuisance (Miller) 3b 2g com sc studio BUU
Nakamitsu (Seami) 5m ext sc Japanese temple CLI
J   Nathaniel Bowditch (Seymour) Nar 8b 2g sc kitchen KON
J   Nativity (Malcolmson) 1b 1g sc stable in Bethlehem MAL
Nature of a gift (Emblem) 7m 6w ext sc stage POW
c   Near Calvary (Richardson) 5b 4g sc in Palestine RIC
c   Near mutiny on the Santa Maria (Carlson) 6b sc on ship CAR
c   Necklace of Princess Fiorimonde (Smith) 12b 5g sc courtyard
SM
c   Needle fights for freedom (MacLellan) Nar 3b 6g sc int DUR

Now we'll play "East Lynn." (Casey) 3m 2w com sc stage BRG
Nude washing dishes (Seiler) 4m 4w com sc int MA4

O

O come to my heart (Sando) any number of characters sc hut
    SAN

c n–r   O little town of Bethlehem (Morley) 9b 3g ext sc village street
    KAN

J n–r   Ode to spring (Hark) 5b 6g sc drug store HAT

J n–r   Odyssey (Homer) Nar 4b 2g ext sc in ancient Greece OLI

Oedipus Rex (Sophocles) 7m 1w chorus sc palace in ancient
    Greece DO

Oedipus the King (Sophocles) 7m 3w chorus sc ancient Greece
    GP

Of gods & man (Fisher) 3m 5w sc library FIU

O'Flaherty, V C (Shaw) 4m 2w voice sc park in Ireland SHA

J   Oh! waitress (Miksch) 3b 2g sc resort hotel MH

Old English Christmas (McDonald) 15m 7w 2b 2g ext sc int
    BRH

J n–r   Old ghosts at home (Murray) 4b 5g sc int BUW

c   Old Glory grows up (Miller) 5m 4w ext sc stage MIF

Old grad (Finch) 3m com sc sheep camp BRI

c n–r   Old King Cole's Christmas (Atherton) 2b 4g sc throne rm KAN

Old lady says "no" (Johnson) 23 characters sc dark glade JOH

Old lady shows her medals (Barrie) 2m 4w sc int BAR FR

c n–r   Old lady witch's party (Very) 4b 6g sc int VE

J   Old lovers ghosts (Murray) 4b 3g sc ghost town hotel MUR

T   Old Mac Donald had a curve (Serling) 21m 1w voice sc base-
    ball SER

Old village school (Sheldon) 2b 6g ext sc int BRJ

c n–r   Old woman & her pig (Very) any number of children sc meadow
    VE

J n–r   Oliver Twist (Dickens) Nar 6b 4g sc English workhouse OLI

J   Oliver Twist asks for more (Howard) Nar 9b 2g ext sc int
    HOW

On Baile's strand (Yeats) 5m ext sc great hall UL

On calvary, a garden (Brown) 7w sc garden BRC

c J n–r   On such a night (Fisher) 4b 1g ext sc int FIR

On the frontier (Pollack) 6m sc Austrian border WAR

c J   On the road to Yorktown (Hughes) Nar 10b sc curtains CI

On vengeance heights (Davis) 2m 2w sc cabin FR

Once a thief (Perrini) 10m 2w sc on a small island MAI

Once upon a Christmas (Chadwicke) 7w sc int FR

c   144 davenports (Stahl) Nar 3b 1g com sc village hotel BRJ

J   One hundred dollars (Murray) 8b 8g com sc int MUR

c   **Parable of the last judgment** (Phillips) 6b voices sc temple PHI

c   **Parable of the Pharisee & the tax collector** (Phillips) 7b sc
        road PHI

       Paradise (Bridie) 1m 6w ext sc booth BR

R   **Paris incident** (Rosten) Nar announcer 6m 1w chorus sc stage
        BAC

       Parliament of heaven (Hegge) 7 characters sc medieval church
        BRT

c n–r **Parrot & the pirates** (Miller) 7b ext sc tropical island MIE

       Parting at Imsdorf (Nusbaum) 4m 1w sc outside FR

J n–r **Part-time hero** (Miller) 2b 4g sc int MIL

       Party through the wall (Spark) Nar 1m 3w sc bombed house SP

       Passing the buck (Pierce) 4w com sc int BRC

       Passion & death of Jesus Christ (Casey) Nar 2m ext sc
        sanctuary CAT

       Passion, Poison, petrifaction (Shaw) 5m 2w sc int SH

c J   **Passover story** (Garvey) 5b 4g sc int CI

T   **Patterns** (Serling) 3m 3w sc Office SER

       Patterson dinner (St. Clair) 6w sc dining rm BRC

c   **Paul Revere** (Kissen) 8b 5g sc colonial int KIS

       Pawns (Wilde) 6m sc Russian int ZA

       Peace is an olive color (Felton) 3m 1b sc int BAK

c   **Pear tree** (McFarlan) 3b 3g sc Chinese market place PLA

J   **Peddler's dream** (Reeves) 6b 6g sc village REE

       Pen is mightier (Victor) 5m sc headquarters WAR

       People in the wind (Inge) 3m 5w sc restaurant IN

       People to people (Martens) 2m 7w sc int BAK

R   **People with light coming out of them** (Saroyan) 6m 2w sc int
        FQ

c   **Peppermint Easter egg** (Slattery) 5b 6g sc throne rm PLA

J R n-r **Perfect couple** (Murray) 5b 5g com sc department store MU

       Perfect gentleman (Joder) 2m 3w com sc int FR

       Period house (Eaton) 3m 5w sc int FR

T   **Perry Como show** (Como) 3m 1w sc television SET

       Petal in the dust (McCoy) 2m 3w sc orchard MCJ

       Peter & the early church (Casey) Nar 6m chorus sc stage CAT

c   **Peter Cottontail** (Francis) 11 characters sc yard FR

       Phantom ship (Matheson) 4w sc cottage EV

       Phoenix too often (Fry) 3m poetic sc tomb FE

       Phormio (Terence) 9m 4w sc ancient Rome CLI

c   **Pictures in the fire** (Martens) 1b 2g sc int BAK

J   **Pilgrim Thanksgiving service** (St. Clair) any number of
        characters music sc church SAI

       Pilgrims progress (Bunyan) many characters sc medieval
        church HL

       Pink & patches (Bland) 1m 3w sc mountains FR

c   Pinky Windy's trip to the moon (Floyd) large case fantasy
         sc stage BAK
J   Pinina goes to Hollywood (Alfiler) 5b 2g sc int EDS
         Pirate king (Brown) 7m ext sc ship BAK
c   Pirate's chest (Pratt) 6b 1g puppet sc int PR
c   Pixie in a trap (Bennett) 7 characters sc woods PLA
c n–r   Planting time (Very) 3b 3g sc outdoors VE
         Play of the shepherds (Wakefield) 3m sc medieval church BRT
         Play of St. George (————) 6m sc medieval church CLI
j   Playful bus (Miksch) Nar 3b 3g com sc bus MH
T   Plenty of rein (Roskam) Nar 2m 2w sc int GUN
         Plot to overthrow Christmas (Corwin) Nar 9m 1w com sc int
         RED
         Plucked peacocks (Provence) 3m sc prison BRI
c   Plum blossom & the dragon (Newman) 2b 7g ext sc fairyland
         PLA
C   Pocahontas (Stahl) Nar 3b 1g sc outdoors BRJ
         Point family (The) (Miller) any number of characters sc
         Sunday school MIZ
J   Poison ivy (DuBois) 5b 3g sc int PLA
c   Polly patchwork (Field) 3b 9g ext sc colonial school FEN OK
         Poor Aubrey (Kelly) 1m 3w com sc int FR
         Popular voice (Housman) 3m 1w sc palace HO
         Portrait (The) (Scala) 6m 6w sc theatre CL2
J n–r   Portrait of an American (Hark) 4b 4g sc int HAT
         Portrait of Nelson Holiday, Jr. (Nall) 5m 5w sc int FR
         Port—Royal (Montherlant) 10m sc monastery HAY
c   Potted Princess (Smith) 9b 5g sc palace SM
J   Prelude to fame (McCaslin) 7b 7g story teller sc New England
         MCB
         Prelude to glory (Bautista) 4m 1w sc int EDM
c n–r   Present from Abe (Newman) 5b 3g sc school rm NEW
R   Price of Free World victory (Wallace) Nar announcer 8m 1w
         BAC
c   Prince & the peddlers (Bennett) 7b 1g sc throne rm PLA
c   Prince & the sleeping beauty (Stahl) Nar 3b 1g com sc Palace
         BRJ
         Prince Boniface discovers Christmas (Sando) any number of
         characters sc castle SAN
         Prince of peace (Gibson) 7m 2w sc int FR
         Princess is sorry (Mijares) 1b 1g com sc int EDS
c   Princess Lonely heart (Miller) 8b 11g sc throne rm MIE PLA
c   Princess too little (Nicholson) 7b 6g sc garden PLA
c   Princess who couldn't cry (Tichenor) 4b 3g puppet sc throne
         rm TI
J n–r   Printer's devil (Dias) 3b 3g com sc principal's office DIA

Prisoner of Zenda (Hope) 9b 1g ext sc int OLI PLA

c n–r Prize shamrock (Newman) 7b 5g ext sc park NEW

J Probable sons (St. Clair) 2b 1g 1c sc int SAI

Professor Cuckoo, crystal gazer (Drummond) announcer 4m com sc stage BRJ

J R Program for peace (Schneideman) Announcer 12b 2g ext sc int SCH

Prologue to an unfinished play (Bridie) 4m sc curtains BR

Prologue to King David (Bridie) 5m 1w sc tent BR

Prometheus bound (Aeschylus) 5m 1w chorus sc desert CLI DO

Promised Messiah (Casey) Nar 7m 2w sc platform CAT

Proof of a man (Love) 4m 2w sc int POX

Property man (Huber) 2m 2w ext com sc stage HU

J Proposal (George) 2b 1g com sc int BRHM

Proposal (Johnson) 2m 3w sc int JO

Protest (Williams) 1b 3w sc Japanese int MCS

Provincial lady (Turgenev) 5m 1w sc Russian int TU

j Pulitzer of "The World" (Reines) 12b 2g sc office RE

Pullman car Hiawatha (Wilder) Nar 4m 4w ext sc stage MOO

c n–r Pumpkineaters' pumpkin (Newman) 1b 1g ext sc meadow NEW

Pure gold (Kaser) Reader 3m 2w com sc stage BRG

Purgatory (Yeats) 1m 1w sc ruined house MOO REH REI UL

Purim dragnet (Segal) 11 roles ext sc headquarters SEF SEG

Purim puppets (Segal) 15 roles voices sc country road SEF SEG

Purple door knob (Eaton) 3w com sc antique store FR

c n–r Puss-in-boots (Very) 10b 1g ext sc mill VR

T Puzzle (The) (Roskan) Nar 3m 1w sc int GUN

Q

c n–r Queen Puff-puff (O'Brien) 2b 3g ext sc int FR

c Queen's flowers (Kissen) 7b 2g sc palace KIR

Quiet please (Biermann) 3m 4w sc cabin DRA

c J R Quiz biz (Murray) 8b 4g ext com sc stage MU

R

c Rabbits who changed their minds (Miller) 3b 1g ext sc forest MIF

T Rack (The) (Serling) 16m 1w sc Pentagon SER

c Racketty- packetty house (Brown) 21 characters sc nursery BRO

c Rainy afternoon (Inge) 1b 2g sc old barn IN

c Rainy day (McCrae) Nar 2b 4g puppet sc int MCR

Ranger takes a wife (Nalasco) 5m 1w sc forest EDS

Road to Bethlehem (Colbey) 3m 6w ext sc hills of Palestine FR
Road to Bethlehem (Gilbert) 7m 6w chorus sc int BRH
Road to Emmaus (Sister M. Francis) 6m 2w sc road FR
c   Robert E. Lee (Kissen) 11b 3g sc int KIS
c J   Robin Hood & the match at Nottingham (Nolan) 8b 2g sc fair NO
Robin Hood in Sherwood forest (Colson) 14b sc forest BUR
Robin-a-tiptoe (Mervale) 7w sc int BAK
Rock (The) (Poole) 4m 2w sc int BAD
Rockers (The) (Johnson) 3m 3w sc rest home JO
J   Rocket of freedom (Fisher) 4m 1g sc int FIS
J   Romance (Hughes) 5w com sc travel bureau DRA
Romance of the willow pattern (Van der Veer) 3m 1w sc int FR
Romeo & Juliet & their papas (McCoy) 2m 2w com sc balcony MOD
Roof (The) (Brenner) 6w sc outside BAK
J n–r   Room for a king (Du Bois) 5b 5g sc yard of an inn HAN
T   Room for death (Hamilton) 6m 3w sc int DAL
J n–r   Room for Mary (Thurston) 6g sc int KAN
Room upstairs (Ramsey) 3m 4w sc int BRI
Roots (Pascual) 1m 3w sc in the Philippines EDM
Rosalind (Barrie) 1m 3w sc parlour BAR
c n–r   Roses for mother (Newman) 2b 3g ext sc garden NEW
c   Rufus Robin's day in court (Rybak) 7b 6g sc garden PLA
Ruling powers (Housman) 3m 2w sc palace in Germany HO
J c   Rumpelstiltskin (Sloane) 9b 3g ext sc outside SL
c   Rumpelstiltskin (Thane) 4b 7g sc hill PLA
J   Runaway (Martens) 14b sc hotel lobby BUU
c   Runaway balloon (McClellan) Nar 2b 3g sc outside DUR
J   Runaway chimney sweep (Somerscales) 9b ext sc int SO
c   Runaway pirate (Bennett) 5b sc harbor BUR DUR
c n–r   Runaway toys (Miller) 6b 6g sc int MIE PLA
c n–r   Runaway unicorn (Miller) 18b 5g sc story book lane MIE

S

c J   S S Tikvah (Segal) 13 characters sc ship cabin SEF SEG
J   Sa pula, sa puto (Rodrigo) 4b 1g sc hut EDS
Sabina (Montano) 5m 5w sc village FL
c   Sacajawea (Kissen) 11b 1g sc Indian camp KIS
Sacrifice of Isaac (Brome) 3m sc outside BRT
c   Safety clinic (Miller) 8b 11g sc waiting rm MIF
c J   Sailing west to find the east (Parsons) 8b 1g sc in Barcelona FEM
c J   Saint (The) (Knowles) 14b 11g ext sc gift shop FR
Saint Joan of the stockyards (Brecht) 14m 3w sc stockyards BF

Seed of Adam (Williams) 8m 4w sc int WIL
Seekers (The) (Greene) 8m sc outside inn POX
Send the light (Miller) 2m sc native hut MIZ
J Sentimental scarecrow (Field) 3b 5g sc field FR
Sermon on the Mount (Casey) Nar 4 singers sc curtains CAT
c J n–r Setting Santa straight (Fisher) 10b 6g sc int FIR
Seven women (Barrie) 2m 3w com sc int FR BAR
Seventeen year old woman (Silverman) 2m 3w com sc int FR
Shadow & solitude (Recto) 3m 3w sc int in Philippines FL
Shadow play (Coward) 5m 4w sc int COW
Shakes versus Shav (Shaw) 3m sc stage SHA
Shall we join the ladies? (Barrie) 8m 8w sc int FR BAR
c J Shavuot day dream (Mittleman) 7b 2g sc int CI
J She laughs last (Paradis) 10w sc bed rm PLA
J T She walks in beauty (Truex) 2m 2w sc suburbs FEI ZA
Shepherd who stayed (Hunter) 4m 2w sc in Bethlehem BRH
Shepherds (Miller) 5m sc church MIZ
J Shepherds play (Malcolmson) 4b 2g infant sc outside MAL
Sheriff (Arnold) 6m 1w sc int FR
Sheriff of Nottingham's nephew (McCoy) 7m com sc forest
MOD
J n–r Sherlock Holmes & the red-headed league (Doyle) 6b outside
OLI
She's from Hollywood (Drummond) 10w sc int BRC
Shewing-up of Blanco Posnet (Shaw) 4m 5w ext sc int SHA
J Shipmates (Fisher) 3b 3g sc int FIS
Shirkers (McLellan) 2m 1w sc int FR
Shirt's off (Huber) 3m 2w com sc curtains HU
C J Shirt-tail boy (Covington) 4b 2g sc cabin IV KON
Shiver my timbers (Murray) 5b 3g com sc aboard ship MUC
PLA
c Shoemaker & the elves (Bennett) 4b 1g sc shop PLA
c n–r Shoemaker & the elves (Very) 6b 2g sc shop VE
Shoemaker's wife (Thompson) 2m 1w com sc medieval int POX
Shoes & stockings & Solomon (Fisher) Reader 3b sc int FIR
Shooting Chanukah (Segal) 10 roles sc conference rm SEF SEG
Short cut (Wilde) 3m sc mine BAK
c Shower of hearts (Miller) 12b 8g sc throne rm MIF
Siege of Calais (Shaw) 5m 1w sc before the walls SHA
c Signpost (Clapp) 4b 2g sc crossroads PLA
Sight for sore thoughts (Stein) 5m 1w sc tavern MA4
c J Silent night (Pauli) 4m sc in Austria OK
Silent watchmen (Segal) 6 roles voice sc house of the scribes
SEF SEG
R Silent woman (Atkins) Nar announcer 9m 7w sc stage BAC
Simple little affair (Herman) 9m 5w sc int FR

J	Some interference! (Miksch) announcer 2b 2g com sc football MH
c n–r	Somebody's valentine (Newman) 3b 5g sc shop NEW
c J n–r	Something in the air (Fisher) 1b 1g sc int FIR
c n–r	Something new for Halloween (Newman) 3b 3g sc cottage NEW
	Something unspoken (Williams) 2w sc southern residence MAI
J	Son of William Tell (Nolan) 8b 3g sc meadow NO
c J R	Song of Queen Esther (Wishengrad) Nar 10 roles sc Palace CI
J n–r	Song of the night (DuBois) 6b 5g sc yard of an inn BUW
	Song of songs (Giraudoux) 7m 1w sc cafe UL
R	Sorry, wrong number (Fletcher) 7m 1w sc int CER FEI NE
	Souls in torment (Tan) 3m 3w 1b sc int EDS
	Sound effects man (Huber) 4m 1w com sc stage HU
	Sound of apples (Young) 6m 3w voices blank verse sc valley MA2
J	Sound punctuation (Miksch) 7 characters com sc school MH
J	Sounds of triumph (Inge) 5m 1w sc college game DRA ZA
c J n–r	Sourdough Sally (Miller) 7b 5g sc Alaska int MIE PLA
J	Spare a copper for the guy! (Pethybridge) 5b 4g sc subway PR
	Sparkin' (Conkle) 1m 3w com sc int FR ZA
c	Special edition (Fisher) 4b 4g sc stage PLA
J	Special services of Mr. Doodle (Murray) 3b 2g com sc int MUR
	Speeches & cream (Tydeman) 10w ext com sc platform BOU4
	Speed, bonnie boat (Wallace) 4m 3w com sc inn POX
	Spirit of Christmas (Harris) any number of characters sc int BRH
	Spirits on parade (McCoy) 2m 2w com sc waiting rm MOD
	Splint for a broken heart (Kirkpatrick) 2m 4w com sc int FR
	Sponsor (The) (Miller) 8m sc church MIZ
	Spreading the news (Gregory) 7m 3w sc Irish fair FR CER
J	Sprig of rosemary (Sloane) 6b 2g sc outdoors SL
J n–r	Spring daze (Hark) 2b 2g com sc int HAT
c	Spunky Punky (Miller) 5b 4g sc garden MIF
c n–r	Squeaknibble's Christmas (Miller) 2b 3g ext sc great hall MIE
c J	Stable at midnight (Fisher) 2b 1g sc stable FIR
c	Staff & the fiddle (Goldsmith) 8b 4g sc house in the woods FEN
J	Stage set for veterans' day (Fisher) 6b 4g sc stage FIS
c J n–r	Standing up for Santa (Fisher) 1b 1g ext sc stage FIS
J n–r	Stanislaw & the wolf (Nolan) 6b 3g sc woods NO
J	Star dust (Miksch) 1b 2g com sc int MH
J	Star for Old Glory (Fisher) 3b 4g sc shop FIS
	Star song (Ryerson) 4m 5w sc inn in Bethlehem FR
c J	Star that never moves (McCaslin) 6b 1g ext story teller sc clearing in the forest MCC
	Starlings (Bridie) 3m sc int BR
c n–r	Stars & stripes (Hark) 4b 2g sc int HAR

Summer conference (Campbell) 2m 6w sc Mt. Olympus MA5
Sun is a dead man's weapon (Carroll) 2m 2w sc int FR
Sunday costs five pesos (Niggli) 1m 4w com sc in Mexico FR
Sunny morning (Quintero) 2m 2w com sc park FR
Sun stroke (Kuekel) 2m 6w com sc sun porch POX
Super light Chanukah (Segal) 10 roles sc open space SEF SED
Superlative relative (Housman) 2m 1w sc drawing rm HO

c   Suppose (Smith) 1b 7g ext sc way to the palace SM
J   Survival (Brenner) 11b 5g sc rooming house KON
c   Susie (Smith) 3b 4g sc after school SMI
c   Susie wonders (Smith) 4b 4g sc outdoors SMI
J   Swank night (Miksch) 3b 3g sc club MH
J   Sweater girls (Miksch) 2b 5g sc int MH
c   Sweet revenge! (Smith) 3b 3g sc outdoors SMI
J   Swiss family Robinson—rescued (Howard) 7b 5g ext Nar Camping HOW
c   Switch-about-shop keepers (Sagoff) 8b 8g sc street PLA
   Syncopated Sedar (Segal) 10 roles sc bus SEF SEG

T

J n–r   Take care, Anne (McCoy) 4b 4g com sc int MCO
J n–r   Take my advice (Murray) 4b 4g com sc editorial office MUC
J   Take-off (Miksch) 2b com sc school MH
c n–r   Talking Christmas tree (Fawcett) 2b 5g sc woods KAN
c n–r   Talking flag (Miller) 9b 6g sc school MIG
c J   Tall Bill & his big ideas (McCaslin) 7b 3g ext sc on the range MCC
c J   Tall, dark & handsome (Smith) 1b 2g sc door step SMI
   Tall grass (States) 5m 2w sc home MA4
J   Tall stranger (Dias) 9m 3w sc hotel lobby PLA
   Taming of a shrew (St. Clair) Nar 7b 2g sc outside tabernacle SAI
   Tarakin (Steinmetz) 3m 3w ext sc in soviet Russia WAR
   Technique is the thing (Medina) 4m 1w sc int EDM
c   Teddy bear hero (Miller 4b 3g ext sc picnic grove MIF
J   Teen-age party (Lynch) 6b 5g ext com sc int FR
   Tell no tales (Huber) 3m 2w com sc doctor's office HU
c   Ten pennies for Lincoln (Miller) 3b 3g ext sc club meeting MIF
   Tenor (The) (Wedekind) 4m 2w sc hotel HUB
J n–r   Ten-penny tragedy (Elfenbein) 4b 4g sc information desk BUU
   Temptation of Christ (York) 3m sc church BRT
   Temptation of Jesus (Phillips) 2b sc wilderness PHI
   Terrible Meek (Kennedy) 2m 1w sc stage FR
c   Terrible Terry's surprise (Boiko) 4b 3g ext sc int PLA
J   Territory is born (Emmons) 26b 2g ext sc outdoors EM
   Terror of light (Williams) 7m 2w sc orchard in Jerusalem WIL

Thou art come to the kingdom (Miller) 2m 3w choir sc church
  MIZ
c Three bears (McCrae) announcer 2b 2g puppets sc int MCR
c Three bears (Sheldon) Nar 1b 4g sc int BRJ
c Three Billy Goats Gruff (Adair) 7 characters puppets sc
  curtains AD
c Three Billy Goats Gruff (Tichenor) 3b 2g puppets sc bridge TI
J Three faces of Easter (Martens) 3b 7g sc stage BAK
c Three little pigs (Adair) 6 characters puppets sc curtains AD
c Three little kittens (Miller) 5b 3g ext sc stage MIF
c n–r Three litttle kittens go to school (Very) 9 characters sc school
  rm VE
  Three Maries (Cornish) 1m 3w sc garden BRT
  Three of them (Drummond) 2m 1w 1b sc int RDM
  Three on a bench (Estrada) 2m 2w com sc park bench POX
  Three people (Gurney) 1m 1w sc university town MAI
  Three rats (Guerrero) 2m 1w sc int FL
c n–r Three sillies (Very) 6b 4g ext sc farmyard VE
J Three skits for Christmas (Emurian) 8b 2g ext sc stage EMM
n–r Three squeals for freedom (Wefer) 2m 4w sc farmhouse JA
  Three Sundays in a week (Poc) 4b 2g sc int PLA
  Three temptations (Williams) 7m 1w chorus sc church WIL
T Three to get married (Hill) 6m 4w sc woods MCS
c n–r Three V's (Hark) 4b 6g ext sc storage warehouse HAR
  Three wayfarers (Hardy) 8m 2w sc cottage MCS
  Three's a crowd (McCarty) 3m 2w com sc park ZA
  Through courage (Estes) Nar 3b ext soloist sc church ES
  Through decision (Estes) Nar 1b ext soloist sc church ES
  Through dedication (Estes) Nar 2b 2g ext sc church ES
  Through divine guidance (Estes) Nar 5b 2g sc church ES
  Through faith (Estes) Nar 6b soloist sc church ES
  Through humility (Estes) Nar 4b 1g soloist sc church ES
J Through Natches Pass (Emmons) 9b 6g ext sc Puget Sound EM
  Through obedience (Estes) Nar 3b ext sc church ES
  Through prayer (Estes) 3b 2g ext sc church ES
  Through prophecy (Estes) Nar 4b 1g ext sc church ES
  Through the holy spirit (Estes) Nar 4b ext voice sc church ES
c Through the looking glass (Brown) 8g commentator sc int BRO
  Through wisdom (Estes) 3b 3g voice sc church ES
  Through with girls (McCoy) 3m 1w com sc int MOD
  Through witnessing (Estes) Nar 4b 1g soloist sc church ES
c Tidings of joy (McFadden) 10b 6g ext sc int FR
T Till death do us part (Hamilton) 3m 1w sc park bench DAL
c Tiniest Christmas tree (Martens) 11 characters ext sc int BAK
c Time machine (Martens) any number of children sc school BAK
  Tiny closet (Inge) 1m 2w sc boarding house IN MA3

Trouble with Christmas presents (Hamlin) 10m 4w com sc int FR

True story of Captain John Smith (Drummond) reader 4b 2g sc stage BRJ

Trysting place (Tarkington) 3b 3g sc resort hotel POE

Tsumansa (Motokiyo) 2m ext sc Japanese int AN

Turn of the century (Gurney) 4m 6w sc living rm MA2

c   Turncoat (Reiner) Nar 5b 2g sc int DUR

Turning point (Gatlin) 3m 2w sc park BRI

Turning the tables (Fisher) 4m 3w sc int FIU

c n–r   Turning the tables (Miller) 15b 10g sc public library MIG

'Twas such a night (Nichols) 4m 3w com sc inn LO

'Twas the night before Christmas (Hendry) 1m 1w sc int FR

J n–r   'Twas the night before Christmas (Pendleton) 3b 2g sc int BUW

J   Twelve days of Christmas (Somerscales) 1b 1g ext sc stage SO

c   Twelve days before Christmas (Wright) many characters sc stage KAN

c n–r   Twelve months (Very) 12b 2g sc int VE

Twelve pound look (Barrie) 2m 2w sc int BAR FR

27 wagons full of cotton (Williams) 2m 1w sc porch CER MOO

c J   23 and Reyna (Citron) Nar announcer 5b 3g sc New York CI

20,000 leagues under the sea (Verne) 8b 1g sc ticket office OLI

Twilight crane (Kinoshita) 4, ext sc Japanese hut NEV

c n–r   Twinkle (Spanner) 4b 5g sc sky KAN

c R   Two boys & a soap box derby (Jackson) 3b 1g voices sc outdoors OK

J n–r   Two for the money (Murray) 5b 8g com sc hotel suit MUC

J n–r   Two for the show (McCoy) 1b 1g com sc int MCO

Two ghosts are better than one (Rider) 5m 1w sc int JA

Two must stay (Lucas) 6w sc on a steamer BOU4

Two sides of darkness (Procunier) 4m 2w ext sc stage MCS MA3

Two women (Russell) 2w sc bed rm EV

Two's company (Perry) 2m 1w sc apartment in New York MA4

Typhus (Dryer) Nar 6m 3w voice sc medieval Italy CJ

U

J T   U F O (Serling) Nar 7m 2w ext sc telephone FEI

Ugly duckling (Milne) 4m 3w voice sc palace CER FR

Umbrellas (Denham) 15w com sc int BAK

Uncle Petey (Courtney) 3m 1w sc park JA

J   Uncle Sam (Emurian) 15b 2g music sc stage EMM

Uncle Santa Claus (McDonald) 3m 3w sc int BRH

Under plain cover (Osborne) 21w ext sc int OS

c n–r   Under the harvest moon (Hark) sc corn field HAR

c J   **Under the skull & bones** (Gow) 9b ext sc quay side FEN
c J   **Unlighted Menorah** (Levinger) 3b 1g sc int CI
T   **Unloved (The)** (Morris) 16m 5w sc drive BAS
       Unto one of these (Miller) Nar 2m 2w sc native hut MIZ
       Unto thy doors (Coyle) 5m 3w sc church POX
       Unwelcome vision (Guder) 3m 1w sc house in Damascus GUD
c J   **Up a Christmas tree** (Fisher) 1m 1w 2b 2g sc int FIR
       Use the book (Huber) 2m 2w com sc int HU
       Used car for sale (Carlino) 3m 1w ext sc used car lot DRA

<h1 style="text-align:center">V</h1>

n–r   **Vacant room** (Morawsky) 1m 3w sc int JA
c   **Valentine box** (Asbrand) large cast sc school rm BAK
J n–r   **Valentine for Kate** (Miller) 4b 5g sc int MIL
c n–r   **Valentine sale** (Very) large cast sc a huge box VE
       Valiant (Hall) 5m 1w sc warden's office ZA
J n–r   **Valiant villain** (Murray) 4b 4g sc cabin MU
       Vashtirama (Segal) 12 roles sc curtains SEF SEG
       Venus beauty factory (Kaser) 14w com sc beauty parlor BRC
       Verdict of one (Kromer) 15m 5w sc stage BAD
       Very cold night (Winnie) 2m voice sc station BAK BAD
c n–r   **Vicky gets the votes** (Miller) 8g 5b sc int MIG
J n–r   **Video Christmas** (Dias) 3b 4g sc int DIA
       View from the bridge (Miller) 10m 3w sc tenement house UL
       Village wooing (Shaw) 3m com sc deck of ship SH
J n–r   **Violets for Christmas** (Kreger) 1b 4g sc office KAN
c   **Violets for Mother's day** (Casey) 4b 4g sc int CAS
       Vision (The) (Grandgeorge) 7m 7w ext sc stage POW
c   **Visit from Washington** (Martens) 2b 1g sc outdoors BAK
T   **Visit to a small planet** (Vidal) 6m 3w ext sc planet CART
       Visit to Birmingham (Housman) 2m 2w sc palace HO
c   **Visit to Goldilocks** (Miller) 2b 3g ext sc woods MIF
J n–r   **Visitor to outer space** (Murray) 7b 8g com sc outer space MUC
       Voice from nowhere (McCoy) 5w com sc int MCJ
       Voices of the Shofarim (Segal) 14 roles sc int SEF SEG
c J   **Vote for Haman!** (Grossman) 5b sc int CI
J n–r   **Vote for Miss Checkout** (Murray) 6b 7g com sc supermarket
         MUC
J n–r   **Vote for your hero** (Hark) 5b 3g sc int HAT

<h1 style="text-align:center">W</h1>

       Wages of sin (Holland) 2m 5w sc int MA5
       Wait (The) (Brenner) 6w sc miner's shack BAK
c   **Wait & see** (Miller) 4b 9g sc int MIF
       Waiter who waited (Huber) 5m com sc restaurant BRJ

c   Wake up Santa Claus (Miller) 6b 3g ext sc Santa's bed rm MIF
Wall (The) (Powers) 5m 2w sc ancient wall POX
Wall (The) (Sando) 2m 2w ext sc wall of Jerusalem SAN
Walls have ears (Segal) 6 roles sc int SEF SEG

J   Walter Scott's American guest (Reines) 5b 1g sc drawing rm
REI
Wandering scholar from Paradise (Sachs) 3m 1w sc outdoors
CLI
Wanted: a ballad (Hopkins) Nar announcer many characters
BAC
Warnings (O'Neil) 4m 1w sc dining rm ON

c n–r   Washington shilling (Miller) 8b 6g sc int MIG

c n–r   Washington's gold button (Newman) 2b 5g sc mansion NEW

c n–r   Washington's leading lady (Miller) 7b 3g sc stage MIG

c n–r   Washington's lucky star (Miller) 5b 5g sc colonial int MIE
PLA

J   Watch the birdie (Miksch) 2b 1g com sc photography studio
MH

c n-r   Way (The) (Runnette) 9b 8g sc inn KAN
Way to the inn (Newman) 5b 5g ext sc home in Bethlehem
NEW PLA
Ways & means (Coward) 5m 4w com sc int COW
We are witnesses (Miller) 1m 3w voices sc church MIZ

c J   We belong (Davis) 25 characters sc class rm CI
We Brents pay our bills (Mannix) 2m 2w sc int BRI
We commit this body (Dace) 6m ext voice sc slave ship MA4

J n–r   We deliver most anywhere (Miksch) 2b 2g com sc super market
MH

c J   We pledge allegiance (Kaplan) 12 characters sc int CI

J   We, the people (Toles) 15b 6g Nar sc stage PLA

c n–r   We want mother (Hark) 2b 2g sc int HAR
Weather or not (Martens) 5b 5g sc weather bureau BAK
Weatherman on trial (Miller) 5b 2g ext sc court rm MIF
Web (The) (O'Neil) 5m 1w sc int ON
Wedding (Chekhov) 6m 3w com sc restaurant FE
Wedding on Eiffel tower (Cocteau) 8m 2w ext sc platform
BEN

c J n–r Week before Christmas (Fisher) 10b 10g sc int FIR
Week before his death (Casey) Nar 1m 2 soloists sc church
CAT
Well (The) (Murray) 3b 3g sc int MUR
Well-remembered voice (Barrie) 2m 2w sc dark rm BAR
Wetback run (Apstein) 15m 1w sc between U. S. & Mexico
MA5
What a classroom! (Kaser) 3m 4w com sc school BRHM
What a game! what a game! (Drummond) reader 2m ext com
sc football field BRJ

Wholesale jealousy (Drummond) 10w sc int BRC

J   Who's for the divide? (Emmons) 2b ext sc int EM

J n–r   Who's old-fashioned? (Hark) 4b 3g sc int HAT

Whosoever believeth (Corrigan) 3m sc Jerusalem FR

c   Why, daddy? (Smith) Nar 2b sc int SMI

Why mothers get gray (Quinlan) 1b 5g sc int QU

Why she would not (Shaw) 5m 1w sc path through a wood
        SHA

Why the chimes rang (McFadden) 3m 1w sc int FR

Wife for a life (A) (O'Neil) 3m sc Arizona desert ON

Wife goes into politics (Ancheta) 3m 2w sc in the Philippines
        MON

Will (The) (Barrie) 6m 1w sc lawyer's office BAR RED FR

T   Will to win (Rodman) 7m 2w Nar sc snow drifting GUN

c   William Penn (Kissen) 13b 4g ext sc street KIS

J   William Tyndal story (St. Clair) 5m Nar sc int SAI

J   Willie's lie detector (Gray) 4b 4g com sc int DRA

Windigo island (Wallerstein) any number of actors sc camp
        WAL

R   Winter cruise (Maugham) 9m 8w sc ship FR

Winter sunset (Brome) 2m 2w sc int BRI

c   Winter wizards (Bennett) 5b 2g sc winter weather PLA

Wire trouble (McCoy) 1m 1w com sc on the telephone MOD

Wise virgins & the foolish virgins (———) 4m sc outdoors
        CLI

c   Wishing stream (Miller) 4b 4g sc stage MIF

c J   With General Wow in darkest Africa (Stahl) 3b 1g com in
        Africa BRJ

With Janet in mind (James) 5w sc English inn BOU7

J n–r   With malice toward none (DuBois) 4b 3g sc int BUW

With sunrise in his pocket (McCaslin) 2 story tellers 2b ext sc
        outside MCC

c   Wizard of Oz (Baum) 6b 6g sc corn field PLA

Woman taken in adultery (Hegge) 6m 1w sc in ancient times
        BRT

Woman's privilege (Hayes) 2m 2w com sc int FR

Women at the well (Guder) 4w sc well GUD

Women in the kitchen (Guder) 1m 4w sc kitchen GUD

Women to remember (Miller) Nar 5w music sc Bible times MIZ

Wondrous gift (Sando) 7m 2b 2g sc lawn SAN

J R   Word (The) (Obler) Announcer 3m 1w sc radio FEI

J n–r   Word of honor (McCoy) 1b 2g com sc antique shop MCO

Workhouse ward (Gregory) 2m 1w sc workhouse in Ireland FR

World is an apple (Florentine) 1m 1w sc street EDM

Worlds apart (Cooper) 4m sc outside BAK

Worming around (McCoy) 2m com sc school MOD

Y

J	Yankee doodle dandy (Fisher) 6b 2g sc backdrop FIS
c J	Yankee peddler (McCaslin) story teller 6b 48 sc country store MCC
	Ye old time vaudeville (Kaser) announcer 3m com sc stage BRHM
J	Yellow fever (Burlingame) 12b sc doctor's office in Cuba BUR
J	Yes means no (Rogers) 3m 2w com sc int DRA
J n–r	You don't belong to me (McCoy) 3b 4g sc int MCO
	You look ghastly (Singsbee) 6w sc hospital BRC
J n–r	You'd never think it (McCoy) 1b 1g com sc int MCO
c R	Young Abe Lincoln (Baker) 4b 4g sc outside OK
J	Young Abe Lincoln (Fisher) 8b 9g sc cabin PLA
J	Young Lochinvar (Somerscales) 2 Nar 4b 2g ext sc int SO
	Young man of means (Guder) 3m 1w sc Jerusalem int GUD
	Young Prince of glory (Brokelsby) large cast sc stage BAK
c	Your mom & my mom (Casey) 5g sc int CAS
n–r	Your rooms are ready (Greene) 5m 1w sc hotel lobby JA
	Your screen test (Sheldon) announcer any number of actors sc stage BRJ
T	You're a long time dead (Morgan) 5m 4w sc dark rm BAS

Z

	Zeal of thy house (Sayers) 27 characters extras sc long time ago HALI
T	Zone of quiet (Lardner) 2m 3w sc hospital SCHR

AUTHORS

A

Abel, Lionel
Death of Odysseus

—

Abraham & Isaac

Adair, Margaret W.
King Midas & the golden touch
Three Billy Goats Gruff
Three little pigs

—

Adam

Adams, Lionel
How the great guest came

Adler, Robert
Open secret

Aeschylus
Prometheus bound

Agee, James
African queen
Blue hotel
Bride comes to yellow sky
Night of the hunter
Noa, noa

Aguirre, Isadora
Express from Santiago

Albee, Edward
Sandbox

Alcott, Louisa M.
Little women

Alderman, Elinor
Anyone for the moon?

Alfiler, Merceder R.
Pinna goes to Hollywood

Allan, Dorothy C.
At the bend of the road

Allensworth, Carl
Simple truth

Allred, Joan
Society page

Allred, Pearl
Orchids for Margaret
To the lovely Margaret

Allyn, Mabel C.
Retrieved Christmas

Return to Berchtesgaden
I saw the lights go out in Europe
I speak for the women of America
Silent women

Atwater, Richard
Mr. Popper's penguins

Auden, W. H.
For the time being

B

Bach, Marcus
Haym Salomon

Bacher, W. A.
Report on the state of the nation

Baleless, Katherine L.
Most memorable

Baker, G. M.
Christmas carol

Baker, Nina B.
Young Abe Lincoln

Banks, Nathaniel
Curate's play

Bannister, Winifred
No tears for Henry

Barbee, Lindsey
Christmas gift
Four in a town

Barksdale, Lena
First Thanksgiving

Barling, Edith M.
The Governor

Barnes, Emily A.
Magic fishbone
Sokar & the crocodile

Barr, June
Lion & the mouse
White Christmas

Barrie, J. M.
Barbara's wedding
Half an hour
New word
Old friends
Old lady shows her medals
Pantaloon
Rosalind
Seven women
Shall we join the ladies
Twelve pound look

Beolco, Angelo
Bilora

Berg, Gertrude
Goldbergs

———

Bird-catcher in Hell

———

Birth of Christ (York)

Bishop, Claire H.
All alone

Blaine, Betty G.
Mother Goose's magic cookies

Bland, Margaret
Pink & patches

Blanton, Catherine
Dulce man

Boiko, Claire
Anywhere & every where
Kitten capers
Terrible Terry's surprise

Bole, Lois E.
Return of the pilgrims

Bollers, G. E.
Jobs for girls

Bolton, Mada G.
Her affairs in order

Booth, Anthony
The notice

Boretz, Alvin
Camp ghost

Box, Muriel
Martha & Mary

Box, Sydney
Not this man

Boyd, James
One more free man

Brackman, Roy
Ready for Robert

Brecht, Bertolt
Good woman of Setznan
Saint Joan of the stockyards

Brenner, Alfred
Survival

Brenner, Marcene
B girls extras
Beacon of strength
Cynthia
The roof
The wait

Bridie, James
Change for the worse
Era of Vincent van Gogh
Fat woman
First scene
Open-air drama
Paradise
Prologue to an unfinished play
Prologue to King David
Scheherazade kept on talking
The starlings

Brides, Ivory
Frozen heart

Brockelsby, Joan
Young prince of glory

Brome, Robert
Bargains in hair cuts
Winter sunset

Brooks, W. R.
Freddy the detective

Brophy, Edmund
Nothin' to nothin'

Brosius, Nancy
A little learning

Broughton, James
Last word

Brown, A. M.
Get along, little cowboy

Brown, Albert
Pirate King

Brown, Alice
Joint owners in Spain

Brown, Madge
On calvary, a garden

Brown, Patricia
Gloria mundi

Brown, Regina
Adventure of Tom Sawyer
Little Princess
Little women
Racketty-packetty house
Through the looking glass
Tom Sawyer's morning

Brydon, Margaret W.
May witch

Buenafe, M.
Resignation
Return of the warrior

Buermann, Howard
Quiet please

Bunyan
Pilgrim's progress
Burdin, Ruth
Miracle for Mary
Burlingame, Cora
Yellow fever
Burnett, F. H.
Little Princess

C

Calitri, P. M.
One love had Mary

Callman, Cecelia C.
Cupid & Co.

Camche, Nancy
Orphans

Campbell, J. G.
Summit conference

Campbell, Josephina E.
St. Patrick's eve

Capell, Loretta C.
First Christmas tree

Carino, Jose
Brown Man's burden

Carlino, L. J.
Junk yard
Mr. Flannery's ocean
Used car for sale

Carlson, Bernice W.
Altogether! Heave!
For soldiers everywhere
Jim Bridger & his eight-hour echo
Near mutiny on the Santa Maria
Traitor's reward

Carlson, Joseph
Bab buys a car

Carlson, Natalie S.
Family under the bridge

Carmichael, Fred
Divorce granted
Green room blues

Carroll, Lewis
Alice in Wonderland

Carroll, P. V.
Beauty is fled
Conspirators
Interlude

Carroll, Robert
Heat lightning

Carroll, R. F.
Sun is a dead man's weapon

Carson, Julia B.
The monster

Carson, W. G. B.
Five for bad luck

Cartwell, V. H.
George

Carver, Juliet
My fair Linda

Case, T. W.
Billy Adams, American

Casey, Arten
Now we'll play "East Lynn"!

Casey, Beatrice M.
All the world loves a mother
The coach
It's tough on mother
Lucky piece for Mom
Mothering Miss Mittie
Violets for Mother's Day
Your Mom & my Mom

Casey, F. J.
Book of Job
Bread of Life
Charity; in the Epistles of
   James & John
Creation sings the glory of God
The family
The good & the evil
"I, Paul—prisoner"
Passion & death of Jesus Christ
Peter & the early church
Promised Messiah
Sermon on the Mount
Week before His Death

Casey, F. M.
Dearie, you're a dreamer
John Shanahan, my boy

Casey, Michael
Soul in fine array

——

Castle of Perseverance

Castro, N. H.
At the turn of the road

Chadwicke, Alice
Once upon a Christmas

Chambers, Van
Beware, Miss Brown, beware
Mother's pet

Chaucer, Geoffrey
Canterbury tales

Chekhov, Anton
The boor
Marriage proposal
A wedding

Chevigny, Hector
Daniel Webster

Chodobov, Stephan
Journal of Vera Grey

Church, Virginia
What men live by

Citron, S. J.
Be not afraid
Eliezer Ben Yehudah
Four Chaplains
Herzl comes home
If not even higher
Jerusalem
Magician
23 and Reyna

Clapp, Patricia
Other side of the wall
Signpost

Clark, B. H.
Fires at Valley Forge

Clemens, Colin
Curtain

Clifford, Vance
Gay nineties barber shop

Climemhaga, Joel
Heathen pioneer

Cocteau, Jean
Wedding on Eiffel Tower

Colbo, Ella S.
Heroine of Wren

Colley, T. D.
Road to Bethlehem

Colman, Ronald
Hall of Ivy

Colson, J. G.
Robin Hood in Sherwood Forest
Top of the hill

Como, Perry
Perry Como show

Conkle, E. P.
Bauble for the baby
China-handled knife
Heaven is a long time to wait
Minnie Fields
Sparkin'

Cummings, Bob
Bob Cummings show

Cummings, E. E.
Santa Claus

Curtis, Agnes
Blackberry pie
Divine spark
Christmas at Mothers

Cutler, Katherine A.
Christmas awakening

D

Dace, Wallace
We commit this body

Daggett, James
Goodnight please

Damico, Jim
Storm is breaking

Dane, Essex
When the whirlwind blows

Daumal, Rene
Engggarrde!

David takes the shoots

David & Bethsheba

Daviot, Gordon
Remember Caesar

Davis, Allan
On vengeance heights

Davis, Moshe
We belong

Death in the tree

Denham, Lillian
Umbrellas

Devany, E. H.
Cow-catcher on the caboose
Red & yellow ark

Dias, E. J.
Beatnik & the Bard
Bow-wow blues
Cast up by the sea
Christmas spirit
Cleanest town in the West
Collector's item
Dear Lottie
General Gage's chowder
Gift of laughter

Just who is crazy?
Love knoweth no bounds
No No a thousand times no!
Professor Cookoo, crystal gazer
Saved in the nick of time
She's from Hollywood
Substitute bride
That's different
True story of Captain John Smith
What a game! What a game!
What a mess
Wholesale jealousy

Dryer, B. V.
Typhus

Du Bois, Graham
Birth place for a King
Daughter of the gods
Everyday is Thanksgiving
Humblest place
Poison ivy
Room for a King
Song in the night
With malice toward none

Dumaual, R. R.
Three of them

Dunlap, R. S.
Salvation of Lonny McCain

Dunphy, Jack
Cafe moon
Too close for comfort

Dunsany, Lord
Jest of Halalaba
Night at an inn

Dunlap, R. S.
Overpraised season

Dustmann, Walter
Indignant ghost

Duthie, Hermine
Wheat fire

Duvall, Lucille M.
Chosen one
Little Chip's Christmas tree

E

Edades, Jean
Juan & the magic fruit

Edmonds, Reba
Guest house, very exclusive

Eastman, Fred
Bread
Doctor decides

Through faith
Through humility
Through obedience
Through prayer
Through prophecy
Through the holy spirit
Through wisdom
Through witnessing

Estrada, Doris
Three on a bench

Euripides
Alcestis

_____

Everyman

_____

Fall of man (York)

_____

Falstaff at Gadshall
Farce of the Worthy Master
Pierre Patelin

F

Farrar, C. O.
Country auction

Faust, J. P.
To us a son

Faux, Domally
Littlest month

Fawcett, Margaret G.
Talking Christmas Tree

Federspiel, Jo Ann
Behold the body

Felsbein, Jerry
Ali Baba & the 40 thieves

Felton, J. W.
Christmas at Check point Charlie
Peace is an olive color

Ferber, Edna
The eldest

Field, Rachel
Fifteenth candle
Polly patchwork
Sentimental scarecrow

Finch, Robert
Desert shall bloom
Goodbye to the Lazy K
Old Grad
Summer comes to the Diamond O

Sing the songs of freedom
Sing the songs of Lincoln
Sing the songs of pioneers
Sing the songs of springtime
Sing the songs of Thanksgiving
Sing the songs of travel
Skills to share
Something in the air
Special edition
Stable at midnight
Stage set for Veterans' Day
Standing up for Santa
Star for Old Glory
Story of a well
Wheels within wheels
Thanks a million
Tree to trim
Trimming the tree
Turning the tables
Up a Christmas tree
Week before Christmas
What happened in Egypt
What happened in Toyland
What is a patriot
What's for Christmas
When freedom was news
Yankee Doodle Dandy
Young Abe Lincoln

Flaten, Mary
Testing ground for democracy

Flather, Horace
Jonathan's day

Fletcher, Lucille
Hitch-hiker
Sorry, wrong number

Fletcher, W. B.
Christmas inside
White table cloths

Florentino, A. S.
Cadaver
The dancers
World is an apple

Flores, A. O.
Blast of the bugle
Scent of fear

Floyd, Barbara
Pinky Windy's trip to the moon

Foley, Marie A.
The gift

Follen, Josephine P.
Alice in Queenland
Count of donkey's island
Evacuation day

Entertaining sister's beaux
Final performance
It might happen
Proposal
So you won't talk!

Gheon, Henry
Christmas in the market place

Gibson, E. L.
Prince of peace

Gibson, William
I lay in Zion

Gilbert, Ann C.
Road to Bethlehem

Gilbert, Craig
End of the story

Gilmore, Alice C.
Lens maker

Gilsdorf, Frederick
Ghost of Benjamin Sweet

Giraudoux, Jean
Song of songs

Glaspell, Susan
Trifles

Godefroy, Vincent
Intermezzo

Golden, John
Clock shop

Goldman, Paul
Mermaid Avenue is the world

Goldsmith, Sophie L.
How boots befooled the King
Staff & the fiddle

Goodman, K. S.
Back of the yards
Dust of the road
Game of chess

Goodman, Patricia
Sauce for the gander

Gould, J. R.
Steps from beyond

Gow, Ronald
Under the Skull & Bones

Gowan, Jane
Smokey wins a star

Grabotov, Boris
Letter from a Red Army man

Graham, Kenneth
Reluctant dragon

Grandgeorge, William
    The vision

Grant, Neil
    Last war

Gray, Virginia H.
    Willie's lie detector

Green, Paul
    Fine wagon
    Fixins'
    Hymn to the rising sun
    In Abraham's bosom
    In the valley
    Last of the Lowries
    Lay this body down
    Lord's will
    Man who died at 12 o'clock
    No 'count boy
    Start in life
    Thirsty heart
    White dresses

Greene, C. G.
    Your rooms are ready

Greene, N. D.
    The seekers

Greene, Robert
    Eliza & the Lexicon

Gregory, Lady
    Rising of the moon
    Spreading the news
    Traveling man
    Workhouse ward

Greth, L. E.
    Ghost from outer space

Grimes, Myrtle McC
    Jeanne D'Arc

Grossman, S. S.
    Vote for Haman!

Guder, Eileen L.
    All in a day's work
    Give us Thursday
    Man with the question
    Status seeker
    This firebrand
    Unwelcome vision
    What child is this?
    Women at the well
    Women in the kitchen
    Young man of means

Guerrero, W. M.
    Three rats

Gurney, A. R.
    Three people
    Turn of the century

H

Hackett, Walter
    Ah, romance
    Facing the future
    Outgoing tide

Hadley, H. I.
    Baby sitters
    Fire in a paper

Haines, W. W.
    Command decision

Hall, Holworthy
    Valiant

Hall, Willis
    Airmail from Cyprus

Hamilton, William
    Room for death
    Till death do us part

Hamlin, Mary P.
    Certain Greeks

Hamlin, Mary P.
    Trouble with Christmas presents

Hammerstein, Oscar
    Getting to know you

Haney, Germaine
    Autograph, please
    Baker's dozen
    Fast finish
    Mrs. Charlie Chan

Hardy, Thomas
    Three wayfarers
    Tony Kytes, the arch deceiver

Hark, Mildred
    Abe Lincoln & little Joe
    Aladdin steps out
    All aboard for Christmas
    All out for Halloween
    Bake a cherry pie
    Book of magic
    Books are bridges
    Bunch of keys
    Boy with a future
    Cabana blues
    Case for books
    Chance to do better
    Christmas eve letter
    Christmas recaptured

Day of thanks
Dinner with the folks
Echo of '76
Enter, George Washington
First in peace
Forest fantasy
Forward march
G for Gettysburg
Glory he deserves
Halloween luck
Heart trouble
Homecoming
House is haunted
If we only could cook
Kindly heart
Knight of safety
Know the truth
Let George do it
Life for mother
Magic egg
Merry Christmas, Crawfords!
Merry Christmas customs
Mind your P's & Q's
Minority of millions
Mom's perfect day
Mother Earth's new dress
Mother's admirers
Mother's V I P's
Neighbors to the north
Ode to spring
Portrait of an American
Reindeer on the roof
Saint Patrick
Spring daze
Stars & stripes
Thanksgiving postscript
Thanksgiving with Uncle Sam
Three V's
To my valentine
Under the harvest moon
Vote for your hero
We want mother
What, no Santa Claus!
What, no venison!
Who's old-fashioned?

Harmer, Mabel
Ghosts on strike

Hare, W. B.
Her Christmas hat

Harmon, D. P.
Melody man

Harper, A. L.
Bundles for Christmas

Harper, J. M.
First cat on Mars

Harris, Claudia L.
Spirit of Christmas

Harris, S. F.
J. Caesar

Harrison, Mary L.
The lesson

Harrity, Richard
Gone tomorrow
Home of the buffalo

Harrowing of hell (York)

Hayden, John
The faithless

Hayes, Marrijane
Woman's privilege

Hayes, Kenneth
Mistress mine

Helburn, Theresa
Enter the hero

Henderson, R. R.
Hot off the griddle

Hendry, Lee
'Twas the night before Christmas

Herman, George
Brighten every corner
Simple little affair

Herman, M. J.
Brother Sam

Herod & the Kings (Coventry)

Hill, Kay
Three to get married

Hoffman, H. G.
Nor long remember

Holloway, Dorothy
Steadfast tin soldier

Holland, Norman
Wages of sin

Homer
Odyssey

Holmes, Ruth V.
In the days of King Alfred
King John & the Abbot of Canterbury

Hope, Anthony
Prisoner of Zenda

Hopkins, Neal
Lesson in Japanese
Wanted: a ballad

Horne, Kay A.
This dark world & wide

Hosking, Nancy K.
Good Ghosts

Houghton, Stanley
Dear departed

Housman, Lawrence
Abraham & Issac
The bell
Domestic difference
Extremes meet
Heavy change
Life in the Highlands
Order of precedence
Popular voice
Recollections
Ruling powers
Superlative relative
This is the heir
Visit to Birmingham

Howard, Helen L.
Ben Franklin, peace-maker
Candles for Christmas
Thankful indeed
What he deserves

Howard, Vernon
Around the world by way of America
David & Goliath
Don Quixote saves the day
Gulliver wins his freedom
Happy holidays for Little Women
Johnny Appleseed in danger
Oliver Twist asks for more
Return of Rip van Winkle
Sir Galahad & the maidens
Strange tale of King Midas
Swiss Family Robinson rescued
Treasure of Monte Cristo

Howe, Grace P.
Grandma

Hsiung, S. I.
Lady Precious Stream

Huber, L. J.
All who enter
Baby hands
Baby sitter
Be careful, Judge
Bent fender
By your hand
Call me dear
Cards on the table
Clean hands
Competition

Days gone by
Defective detective
Do I bother you?
Don't cry, baby
Fight to a finish
Fountains of youth
Free samples
Herbert's hurt
Hurry, Doctor
I'm not here
In union
Innocent bystander
It's a silly game
Kill the Ump
Let's modernize
Let's pretend
Love's labor
Male, model
Man of many miens
Medicine man
Mills that grind
Mother remembers
Newspaper nightmare
Order in the court
Outcome of income
Property man
Reversal in rehearsal
School daze minstrels
Shirt's off
Some fun, son
Sound effects man
Stay awake
Tell no tales
Use the book
Waiter who waited

Hughes, Babette
Mrs. Harper's bazaar

Hughes, Glenn
Red carnations
Romance

Hughes, Ken
Sammy

Hughes, Rupert
On the road to Yorktown

Hugo, Victor
Bishop's candlesticks
Christmas for Cosette

Hunter, Stuart
Shepherd who stayed
Sod

Hunterton, M.
Headless horseman

K

Tree that wanted new leaves
William Penn

Kjelgaard, James
Danny meets Big Red

Klein, Murial W.
Ali Baba & the 40 thieves

Kleinsinger, George
Archy & Melitabel

Kneale, Nigel
Mrs. Wickens in the fall

Knowles, A. B.
The saint

Knox, Florence K.
For distinguished service

Konick, Marcus
Forbidden Christmas

Kozlenko, William
Jacob comes home
Journey of promise

Kraft, H. S.
Bishop of Munster

Krige, Uys
All roads lead to Rome
The arrest
Fuente sagrada
The sniper

Kromer, Helen
Verdict of one

Kruckemeyer, Erna
And he came to his father

Kuekel, W. A.
Sunstroke

L

Lagerkvist, Pai
Let man live

Laidlaw, George
Command decision

Lamb, P. J.
Go down Moses

Lampell, Mildred
Lonesome train

Lardner, Ring
Tridget of Greva
Zone of quiet

Larkin, Margaret
El Christo

Larson, Edith
Christmas bug

———

Last judgment (York)

Latham, J.
One in twelve

Latouche, John
Mrs. Murgatroyd's dime
Statue of Liberty

Lawrence, D. H.
David

Lawrence, Jerome
Inside a kid's head

Learsi, Rufus
Bar Giora
To the young, a vision

Lee, Margaret
Dope

Lehman, Gene
Ghost of laughing Dan

Lehman, Leo
30 pieces of silver

Leuser, Eleanor D.
Christmas sampler
Five brothers
Honored one
Legend of the Christmas rose
Magic well

Levinger, Elma E.
Unlighted Menorah

Lewis, Mary R.
Dick Whittington

Lindsay, Henry
Forever Judy

Lindley, Valrose
Easy exit
Open door

Longreth, Edward
Golden touch

Lord, Katherine
Greatest gift

Love, C. R.
Proof of a man

Lowe, Margaret
Girdle around the world

Lucas, Victor
Two must stay

Hospital blues
How we started
If thoughts could speak
Instructions for Gary
Johnny Nightmare
Keep it under cover
Kupid's college
Luncheon for three
Mary Anne's mortgage
Miss Fix-it
Nerve on display
No threat for Gilbert
One timetable
Petal in the dust
Really significant poem
Romeo & Juliet & their papas
Sheriff of Nottingham's nephews
She's not talking
Social climbing
Spirits on parade
Take care, Anne
Through with girls
Tragedy in rhyme
Two for the show
Voice from nowhere
What's in a name?
Wire trouble
Word of honor
Worming around
You don't belong to me
You'd never think it

McCrea, Lillian
Betty & her friends
Betty's birthday
Betty's surprise
David's rabbits
A dog for Betty
Father Christmas
Little Red Riding Hood
Mother hen
Mummy's secret
Rainy day
Story of Christmas
Three bears

McDonald, Dora M.
Christmas miracle
Old fashioned English Christmas
Uncle Santa Claus

McFadden, Elizabeth
Boy who discovered Easter
Dragon who giggled
Tidings of joy
Why the chimes rang

McFall, Eve
Case against Eve

McFarlan, Ethel
Pear tree

McGanghan, Geraldine
Afterwards

McGowan, Jane
Admiral's nightmare
Christmas every day
Coming of the Prince

McKinnel, Norman
Bishop's candlesticks

McLaughlin, Miriam
Mind's construction

MacLeish, Archibald
The admiral
Fall of the city
Ripe strawberries
States talking
This music crept by me over the waters

McLellan, C. M. S.
Shirkers

MacLellan, Esther
Needle fights for freedom
Return of the Nina
Runaway balloon
Small shoes & Small tulips

McMahon, Luella E.
First Mrs. Paris

McMullen, J. C.
Buddie buys an orchid
Counting the calories
Gifts of St. Patrick

Macneice, Louis
Administrator
Mad island

M

Mack, Rachel
Agustina of the lightheart
Christina goes by with goats

Magee, J. G.
High flight

Malcolm, Ian
This gentlemen, is justice

Makowsky, Lucile
New world

Malcolmson, Anne
Abraham & Issac
Herod & the magi
The nativity

Maurette, Marcelle
Recognition scene from Anastasia

Medcraft, Russel
First dress suit

Medina, A. E.
Technique is the thing

Merivale, Bernard
Robin-a-tiptoe

Mijares, J. M.
Princess is sorry

Miksch, W. F.
Affair in the park
Afternoon at Central station
Anybody's gift
Art alliance
Back seat pilot
Big hunt
Blind date
Camp Crowhill here we come
Craftsman
Dancing lessons
Dates are big business
Day of departure
Daylight saving
Emergency Doctor
End of the line
Entertainment Com'n.
Evening bells
Expanding trade
First aid without aiding
Help wanted—badly
Helping hand
Holiday homecoming
Hollywood horseplay
House guest
How to study
I want a policeman
Idol worshipers
Is thrift a virtue?
It's no picnic
Keep smiling
Life is so dull
Negations
Oh! waitress
Out in the rain again
Playful bus
Science is wonderful
Sitting tonight
Soloist
Some interference!
Sound punctuation
Star dust
Subscribe now
Swank night

Mary's invitation
Mayday for mother
Meet Mr. Muffin
Melody for Lincoln
Merry-go-round for mother
Miraculous tea party
Mistletoe mystery
Monsieur Santa Claus
Mother beats the band
Mother goose bake shop
Mother's fairy godmother
Mother's hidden talent
Mouse that soared
Mr. Snow White's Thanksgiving
Mystery of Knob Creek farm
Mystery of Turkey-Lurkey
N for nuisance
New shoes
Old Glory grows up
Parrot & the pirates
Part-time hero
Princess Lonely Heart
Rabbits who changed their minds
Real Princess
Red carpet Christmas
Red flannel suit
Runaway toys
Runaway unicorn
Safety clinic
Santa Claus for President
Santa Claus twins
School for scaring
Season's greetings
Shower of hearts
Smokey wins his star
So long at the fair
Soft-hearted ghost
Softy the snow-man
Sourdough Sally
Spunky Punky
Squeaknibble's Christmas
Strictly Puritan
Talking flag
Teddy bear hero
Ten pennies for Lincoln
Thanks to butter-finger
Thanksgiving riddle
Thankful's red beads
Three little kittens
Tree of hearts
Trouble in Tick-Tock town
Turning the tables
Valentine for Kate
Vicky gets the votes
Visit to Goldilocks
Wait & see
Wake up Santa Claus

Montherlaut, Henry de
  Port-Royal

Moore, Garry
  Garry Moore show

Moore, Lidian
  Christmas at the Gables

Moore, W. H.
  Magic box

Morawsky, Maria
  Vacant room

Morgan, Elaine
  You're a long time dead

Morley, Olive J.
  Little women
  O little town of Bethlehem

Morris, Colin
  The unloved

Morris, T. B.
  Apple-pie order
  Check to the Queen
  Druid's ring
  Everybody comes to Mabel
  Red herrings
  White queen, red queen

Mortimer, John
  Call me a liar

Mosel, Tad
  Five dollar bill
  Impromptu
  Jinxed

Motokiyo, S.
  Atsumori
  Dwarf trees
  Heavenly robe of feathers
  Kagekiyo
  Tsnemasa

Mueller, D. A.
  Eyes upon the cross

Murdock, Marion
  The cuckoo

Murray, John
  Badlands ballyhoo
  Belles of Horsefly Gulch
  Colossal, stupendous!
  Broomstick beauty
  Case of mistaken identity
  Don't call us—We'll call you
  Enie, meenie, minee, murder!
  Every room with bath
  Gray flannel blues

Portrait of Nelson Holiday, Jr.
Touch of fancy

Neikirk, Mabel E.
Oscar on rolling skates

Nelson, Harriet
Adventures of Ozzie & Harriet

Neuenburg, Evelyn
Charm racket
Distant thunder
Fear in a murderer
Fog
Invisible **key**

Newman, Deborah
Aladdin
All America tour
Best part of Christmas
Bunny of the year
Christmas at the Cratchits
Christmas tree surprise
Compass
Election day in the USA
Emperor's new clothes
Fire-safe town
First Thanksgiving
Gift to the world
Happy holidays
In honor of trees
Keys to peace
Long ago in Bethlehem
Magic goose
Memorial day for the blue & the gray
Mr. Lincoln's beard
New Washington
Present for Abe
Prize shamrock
Plum Blossom & the dragon
Pumpkin-eaters pumpkin
Real Princess
Roses for mother
Somebody's valentine
Something new for Halloween
Stolen heart
Stars & stripes
Thanks for Thanksgiving
Thanks to the Indians
Washington's gold button
Way to the inn

Nichols, Jane
'Twas such a night

Nicholson, Jessie
Holiday for Santa
Mind over matter

O'Brien, Seumas
Queen Puff puff

O'Casey, Sean
Bedtime story
Figuro in the night
Moon shines on Kylenamoe

O'Hara, Peggy
Mrs. Murphy's chowder

Olfson, Lewy
Birds' Christmas carol
Christmas coast to coast
Infanta

Oller, Marie
Apple of discord

Olson, E. E.
They say ———

O'Neill, Eugene
Abortion
Bound East for Cardiff
Emperor Jones
Fog
Ile
In the zone
Long journey home
Moon of the Caribbees
Movie man
Reckless
The sniper
Thirst
Warnings
The web
A wife for a life

Orme, Frank
Graduation present

Osborn, Paul
Madame Curie

Osborne, John
Under plain cover

Ouzts, Joyce D.
Happy pagan
Just a picture

P

Paar, Jack
Jack Paar show

Palarca, Julai
Other tomorrows
———
Palm Sunday (York)

Pethybridge, D. C.
Daughter of Pharaoh
Red cord
Spare a copper for the guy!

Phelps, Franklin
Henry, the model husband
King's toemain
Sudden riches

Phelps, Lyon
Gospel witch

Phelps, Pauline
Christmas rose

Phillips, Ernestine
Aesop, man of fable

Phillips, J. B.
Arrest in the garden
Ascension
Baptism of Jesus
Boyhood of Jesus
Calling of the disciples
Centurion's servant
Christ enters Jerusalem
Christ the son of God
Cleansing of the Temple
Death of Jesus
Gift of the holy spirit
Healing at the pool of Bethsheba
Healing of the man born blind
Healing of the paralyzed man
Jesus appears in Galilee
Jesus appears to his disciples
Jesus returns to Galilee
Journey to Jerusalem
Last supper
Lord's prayer
Parable of the last judgment
Parable of the Pharisee & the tax
        collector
Resurrection of Jesus
Temptation of Jesus
Transfiguration
Trial before Pilate

Phillips, J. J.
Light on Slane

Phillips, Margaret K.
Ever on Christmas eve
Man behind the book
Violets for Christmas

Pierce, C. W.
Passing the buck

Pinget, Robert
Architruc

Pirandello
Man with the flower in his mouth

Pitner, Monty
The decision

Plautus
The captives
———

Play of St. George
———

Play of the shepherds (Wakefield)

Pollock, John
On the frontier

Poe, E. A.
Three Sundays in a week

Pool, Alan
The rock

Potter, Dan S.
Touch of marble

Poverman, Helen
Easy money

Powers, Verne
The wall

Pratt, Lois
Goldilocks & the three bears
Little bear tries to see Santa Claus
Pirates chest

Preston, Effa E.
A Greene Christmas
Knight before Christmas
Memory saving time
Merry Christmas in the old home town
Mrs. Bates at the PTA
What's trumps?

Price, Leland
Bessie, the bandit's beautiful baby
City slicker & our Nell
Desperate Desmond's dastardly deed
Fanny, the farmer's daughter
For his brother's crime

Price, Olive
Family tree

Procunier, E. R.
Two sides of darkness

Provence, Jean
Don't get excited
Hat
His sister
Not for credit
Operations
Plucked peacocks

Reason enough
Statistics

Purkey, Ruth A.
Hangs over thy head
Leprechaun
Let go the dream

Pyle, Mary T.
Not on the menu

Q

Quambao, E. A.
The papers

Quinlan, M. Eva
Boston Tea Party
Dorothea dances the minuet
Final rehearsal
Hiding place
Pan of candy
Why mothers get gray

Quinn, A. H.
Ball of St. Hildegards

Quinn, Carolyn
For want of a character

Quintero, Serfin
Sunny morning

R

Ramsey, Helen
Room upstairs

Ratcliff, Nora
Daughters of invention

Rattingan, T.
Browning version

Raye, Martha
Martha Raye show

Reach, James
Fright
His first date

Recto, C. N.
Shadow & solitude

Rees, Phoebe M.
Idols
Sanctuary

Reeves, James
Mulcaster market
Peddler's dream
Stolen boy

Robinson, M. G.
Dr. Heidegger's experiment

Rodman, Howard
Faith hawker
Thing of beauty
Will to win

Rodrigo, F.
Sa pula, sa puto

Rospke, Gabriela
White butterfly

Roer, Bernice
Charmed, I'm sure

Rogers, H. E.
Yes means no

Rogers, J. W.
Judge Lynch

Rojo, T. A.
At stake
Living dead men

Rose, Reginald
Almanac of liberty

Roskam, Clara
Plenty of rein
Puzzle

Rosten, Norman
Ballet of Bataan
Miss Liberty goes to town
Paris incident

Royce, Bon
Bill the matchmaker

Runnette, Helen V.
Touchstone
The way

Russcoll, Joseph
Awakening of Johnny Castle
Modern Scrooge

Russell, Ivy
Second thought

Russell, Eileen
All quiet in the air
Two women

Rybak, Rose K.
Day the moonmen landed
Rufus Robin's day in court

Ryerson, Florence
Albuquerque ten minutes
Double date

Prince Boniface discovers
The wall
Wondrous gift

Saroyan, William
Hello out there
People with the light coming out
of them

Sartoris, Ramon
Clue to the wrong thing
From core to rind
If Caesar be

Sauer, Julia L.
Light on Tern Rock

Savage, G. M.
Little prison

Sayers, Dorothy
Zeal of thy house

Sayre, G. W.
Final edition

Scala, Fliminio
The portrait

Scheville, James
Bloody tenet

Schneideman, Rose
Best citizens of our town
Change of mind
Crossroads to education
Hands across the sea
Love your neighbor
Melting pot
No-tax island
Program for peace
Santa strikes back
Soldiers of peace
This is New York

Scholl, Ralph
Golden axe

Seami
Nakamitsu

———
Second shepherd's play
———
Second trial before Pilate

Segal, S. M.
Achash Veros, incorporated
Chanukah lights & satellites
Chanukah on a mystery planet
Clock that rested
Great charoses
It happened on Kol Nidre night
Kite fell in the sukkah

Sheldon, G. E.
At home with the range
Crime club
Fatal scream
The ham that am
In the land of schmozz
Inconsequential journeys
Little Red Riding Hood
Missing false teeth
Musical answers
Nobody knows
Old village school
Still in the night
Three bears
Whole famdamily
Your screen test

Sheridan, R. B.
The rivals

Sherwood, R. E.
Abe Lincoln in Illinois
American crusader

Shively, Josephine
Christmas eve dream

Shore, Maxine
Catastrophe Clarence

Sicam, F.
Cowards die a thousand deaths
Mir-I-Nisa

Silverman, Irving
Seventeen year old woman

Simon, Irving
Ghosts a la mode

Singsbee, Esther G.
Her majesty comes home
You look ghastly

Simonds, Natalie
Hansel & Gretel

Sister Mary Frances
Road to Emmaus

Sister M. Genevieve
Christmas in the Mountain chapel
A court, a Queen & the church
Seasons come & go

Slattery, Margaret
Golden hearts
Peppermint Easter egg

Sloane, Gertrude L.
Golden goose
King Thrushbeard
Little red hen

Runaway chimney sweep
Toy's revolt
Twelve days of Christmas
Trial of the faithful
Young Lochinvar

Sophocles
Antigone
Oedipus Rex
Oedipus the King

Spanner, Claribel
Twinkle

Spark, Muriel
Danger zone
Dry river bed
Interview
Party through the wall

Stahl, Le Roy
Mail order dragon
One hundred & forty-four davenports
Pocahontas
Prince & the sleeping beauty
With General Wow in darkest Africa

Standt, Edward
Cabbages

States, Bert O.
Tall grass

Stearns, Mary
Diet begins tomorrow

Steele, Daniel
Giant stair

Steele, Sidney
First rehearsal
Have a good time
It's her or the car
Lone hunt

Stein, Howard
Sight for sore thoughts

Steinitz, Martha
Tarakin

Stevens, H. B.
Lincoln reckons up

Stockton, Richard F.
Fabulous tale

Stoler, S. A.
Ghost by request

Stone, J. F.
Where is my wandering boy tonight

Strindberg, August
Creditors

Tickenor, Tom
    City mouse & country mouse
    Little red hen
    Princess who couldn't cry
    Three Billy Goats Gruff

Toles, Myriam
    We, the people

Tolstoi, Leo
    What men live by

Totheroh, Dan
    Emperor's nightingale
    Lost Princess
    Stolen Prince

Truck, O. R.
    The frontier

Truex, James
    She walks in beauty

Tunick, Irve
    Medal for Miss Walker

Turgenev, Ivan
    Provincial lady

Turner, W. P.
    Christ in Concrete City

Tydeman, Richard
    Speeches & cream

U

Urban, Catherine
    Alice in Bookland
    Mrs. Claus' Christmas present
    Santa & the Spacemen
    Who started the fire

V

Valency, Maurice
    Apollo of Bellac
    Feathertop
    Second stranger

Van der Veer, Ethel
    Romance of the willow pattern

Van Druten, J.
    I remember mama

Very, Alice
    Abe Lincoln goes to school
    The callers
    Cat who wanted to ride
    Cock & the fox
    Dancing children

Wallerstein, J. S.
 Bobby & the time machine
 Cactus wild cat
 Johnny Aladdin
 Windigo island

Walsh, Norman
 Let there be farce

Wasserman, Dale
 Elisha & the Long Knives

Watts, A. S.
 As moths unto the lamp

Watts, Frances B.
 Crimson feather

Webb, Barbara
 Christmas star for Olga

Webb, Charles
 Lawyer Lincoln

Weber, W. L.
 Miracle of the boar

Wedekind, Frank
 The tenor

Wefer, Marion
 A gift twice given
 King shall reign
 Three squeals for freedom

Weinstock, David
 Dawn to come

Welch, Rae
 Let's get out of here

Welff, Eric
 Ghost of Caesar's hair

Welles, Orson
 His honor, the mayor

Wells, H. G.
 Invisible man

Werner, Sally
 Home, sweet home

West, Margaret K.
 Madame Dode

Wiggins, Kate D.
 Bird's Christmas carol

Wilde, Oscar
 Florentine tragedy

Wilde, Percival
 Affair of dishonor
 Bow to lotta
 Comrades in arms
 Enchanted Christmas tree

Wolfe, Thomas
Face of America

Wolman, Diana
Imaginary trial of George Washington

Wong, Benjamin
Best way to die

Worchester, Natalie S.
Mad tea party

Woskoff, Verna
Castle in the village

Woman taken in adultery (Hegge)

Wright, Doris G.
Twelve days of Christmas

Wright, Lula
Mr. Poppers penguins

Y

Yeats, W. B.
Cathleen ni Houlihan
Land of Heart's desire
On Baile's strand
Purgatory
Young, Stanley
Sound of apples

Yost, Dorothy
No room at the inn

Z

Zeiger, Henry
Five days

Ziemer, Gregor
Education for death

Zion, Joel
To the new world

Zuckerman, A. J.
Blobo's boy

Zweig, Esther S.
Holiday minstrels

COLLECTIONS

A

Adair, Margaret W. Do-it-in-a-day puppets. N. Y. Day, 1964.
King Midas & the golden touch
Three little pigs
Three Billy Goats Gruff
Also material on puppets

Agee, James. On film. vol. 2. N. Y. McDowell, 1960
"Noa Noa"
African queen
Night of the hunter
Bride comes to Yellow Sky
Blue hotel

Anderson, G. L. ed. Masterpieces of the Orient. N. Y. Norton, 1961.
Motokiyo, Seami—Atsumori
Motokiyo, Seami—Dwarf trees
Motokiyo, Seami—Heavenly robe of feathers
Motokiyo, Seami—Kagekiyo
Motokiyo, Seami—Tsunemasa
Also material on the Near East, India & Japan.

B

Bacher, W. A. ed. Treasury Star parade. N. Y. Farrar, 1942.
Hopkins, Neal. Wanted: a ballad
Rosten, Norma. Ballad of Bataan
Benet, S. V. Nightmare at noon
Latouche, John. Mrs. Murgatroyd's dime
Ziemer, Gregor. Education for death
Atkins, Violet. Education for life
Atkins, Violet. Education for victory
Ruscoll, Joseph. Awakening of Johnny Castle
Fowler, Gene. Jarvis Bay
Magee, J. G. High flight
Atkins, Violet. I saw the lights go out in Europe
Wolfe, Thomas. Face of America
Rosten, Norman. Paris incident
Grabotov, Boris. Letter from a Red Army man
Atkins, Violet. Return to Berchtesgaden
Gallico, Paul. Snow goose
Atkins, Violet. I speak for the women of America
Ruscoll, Joseph. Modern Scrooge
Atkins, Violet. Silent women
Bacher, W. A. Report on the state of the nation

Rosten, Norman. Miss Liberty goes to town
O'Brien, H. V. So long son
Mann, Thomas. Christmas Letter to the German people
Obler, Arch. Chicago, Germany
Kraft, H. S. Bishop of Munster
Latouche, John. Statue of Liberty
Hopkins, Neal. Lesson in Japanese
Wallace, H. A. Price of world victory

Bachman, J. W. & Browne, E. M. Better plays for today's churches. N. Y. Association, 1964.
McFall, Eve. Case against Eve
Kromer, Helen. Verdict of one
Swann, D. L. Circle beyond fear
Turner, D. L. Christ in Concrete City
Winne, D. J. Very cold night
Poole, Alan. The rock
Mueller, D. A. Eyes upon the cross
Gheon, Henri. Christmas in the market place
Banks, Nathaniel. Curate's play
Housman, Lawrence. Abraham & Isaac
Lamb, P. J. Go down Moses
    Also a longer play.

Barrie, J. M. Plays of J. M. Barrie. N. Y. Scribner, 1952.
Pantaloon
Half an hour
Seven women
Old friends
Rosalind
The will
Twelve-pound look
New word
Well-remembered voice
Barbara's wedding
Old lady shows her medals
Shall we join the ladies?
    Also 7 full length plays.

Barry, Michael. Television playwright. N. Y. Hill & Wang, 1960.
Hughes, Ken. Sammy
Hall, Willie. Airmail from Cyprus
Kneale, Nigel. Mrs. Wickens in the fall
Wilson, Donald. Flight of the dove
Voysey, Michael. Amorous goldfish
Lehman, Leo. 30 pieces of silver
Morgan, Elaine. You're a long time
Mortimer, John. Call me a liar
Morris, Colin. The unloved

Becker, R. G. Plays for our time. N. Y. Oxford, 1959.
Haines, W. W. Command decision

Osborne, Paul. Madame Curie
Corwin, Norman. Ann Rutledge
    Also longer plays for radio, television & motion pictures.

Beckett, Samuel. End game; Act without words. N. Y. Grove, 1958.

End game
Act without words

Beckett, Samuel. Krapp's last tape & other dramatic pieces. N. Y. Grove,
    1960.

Krapp's last tape
All that fall
Embers
Act without words I
Act without words II

Benedikt, Michael & Wellwarth G. E. Modern French theatre. N. Y.
    Dutton, 1964.

Cocteau, Jean. Wedding on Eiffel tower
Aragon, Louis. Mirror-wardrobe one fine evening
Salacrou, Armant. Circus story
Daumal, Rene. Engggarrde!
Artaud, Antonin. Jet of blood
Anouilh, Jean. Humulus the mute
Tardieu, Jean. One way for another
Pinget, Robert. Architruc
Ionesco, Eugene. The painting
    Also longer plays.

Bentley, Eric, ed. From the modern repertoire. Series 3. Bloomington,
    Indiana Uni., 1956.

Musset, Alfred de. Door should either be open or shut
Brecht, Bertolt. Saint Joan of the stockyards
Anouilh, Jean. Cecile
Jeffers, Robinson. Cretan woman
    Also long plays & other material.

Bourne, John, ed. New play annual for women. No. 4. London, Evans,
    1959.

Peach, L. DuG. Four queens wait for Henry
Gordon, Patricia. Sauce for the gander
Booth, Anthony. The notice
Lucas, Victor. Two must stay
Tydeman, Richard. Speeches & cream
    Also one longer play.

Bourne, John, ed. New play annual for women. No. 7. London, Evans,
    1963.

English, Arnold. Miss Tarzan into space
John, James. With Janet in mind
Bartlet, Joyce. The gentle push
    Also longer play.

Bridie, James. Tedious & brief. London, Constable, n.d.

Prologue to an unfinished play
Change for the worst
First scene
Open-air drama
Era of Vincent van Gogh
Scheherazade kept talking
Prologue to King David
Paradise
Fat woman
Starling
 Also other material.

Bright, F. R. & Potter, Ralph. To be an American. Philadelphia, Lippincott 1957.

McLeish, Archibald. The admiral
McLeish, Archibald. Ripe strawberries & gooseberries
McLeish, Archibald. Sweet single roses
 Also other material.

Brings, L. M. ed. Clubwoman's entertainment book. Minneapolis, Denison, 1957.

Provence, Jean. Don't get excited
Provence, Jean. Hat
Huber, L. J. Herbert's hurt
Provence, Jean. His sister
Preston, Effie E. Memory saving time
Preston, Effie E. Reason enough
Preston, Effie E. Statistics
Singsbee, Esther G. You look ghastly
Preston, Effie E. What's trump
Chambers, Van. Beware, Miss Brown
Drummond, Richard. Box of trouble
Drummond, Richard. Cleopatra, the second
Huber, L. J. In union
Drummond, Richard. Just who's crazy
Donovan, Alice. Meeting to music
Chalmers, Van. Mother's pet
Drummond, Richard. She's from Hollywood
Drummond, Richard. Wholesale jealousy
Drummond, Richard. Anything to get votes
Haney, Germaine. Autograph please
Haney, Germaine. Baker's dozen
Curtis, Agnes. Blackberry pie
Huber, L. J. By your hand
Roer, Bernice. Charmed, I'm sure
Curtis, Agnes. Divine spark
Haney, Germaine. Fast friends
Huber, L. J. Mother remembers
Haney, Germaine. Mrs. Charlie Chan
O'Brien, Gladys. Mystery manor

Brown, Madge. On Calvary, a garden
Pierce, C. W. Passing the buck
St. Clair, Robert. Patterson dinner
Brackman, Roy. Ready for Robert
Kaser, A. L. Venus beauty factory
    Also a pageant and 2 pantomimes.

Brings, L. M. comp. Gay nineties melodramas. Minneapolis, Denison, 1963.
Drummond, Richard. Saved in the nick of time
Drummond, Richard. Love knoweth no bounds
Drummond, Richard. Foiled again, or, saved by fate
Drummond, Richard. For the land's sake!
Drummond, Richard. In the nick of time
Drummond, Richard. The elopement
Kaser, A. L. Dark doings at the crossroads
Kaser, A. L. Out of the storm
Kaser, A. L. Stolen submarine
Kaser, A. L. Gay nineties fun
Kaser, A. L. Captain Kidd's kid
Kaser, A. L. Pure gold
Kaser, A. L. Tragedy of the sea
Kaser, A. L. A thief in the house
Kaser, A. L. The lowly milkman
Kaser, A. L. When the West was young
Price, Leland. City slicker & our Nell
Price, Leland. For his brother's crime
Price, Leland. Fanny, the farmer's daughter
Price, Leland. Desperate Desmond's dastardly deed
Price, Leland. Bessie, the bandit's beautiful baby
Stone, J. F. Where is my wandering boy tonight
Donald, Helen. Innocence triumphs
Casey, Arten. Now we'll play "East Lynn!"

Brings, L. M. ed. Golden book of Christmas plays. Minneapolis, Denison, 1962.
McCoy, P. S. Christmas barricade
Shively, Josephine. Christmas eve dream
Curtis, Agnes. Christmas at mothers
Barbee, Lindsey. Christmas gift
McDonald, Dora M. Christmas miracle
Phelps, Pauline. Christmas rose
Johnson, F. G. Christmas that bounced
Preston, Effie E. A Greene Christmas
Hare, W. B. Her Christmas hat
Preston, Effie E. Knight before Christmas
Preston, Effie E. Merry Christmas in the old home town
Roberts, Helen M. No more Christmas
Allyn, Mabel C. Retrieved Christmas
Mattson, Jean M. Search for the Savior
Gilbert, Ann C. Road to Bethlehem

Crouch, Mabel. Where's your Christmas spirit?
Hunter, Stuart. Shepherd who stayed
Cutler, Katherine. Christmas awakening
Harris, Claudia L. Spirit of Christmas
McDonald, Dora M. Uncle Santa Claus
McDonald, Dora M. An old English Christmas
James, E. P. Gift of music

Brings, L. M. comp. Master stunt book. Minneapolis, Denison, 1956.

Clifford, Vance. Gay nineties barber shop
Drummond, Richard. Bachelor husbands
Drummond, Richard. Curtain time
Drummond, Richard. No, no, a thousand times no!
Drummond, Richard, That's different
Fisher, Aileen L. Dr. Killemquick's medicine show
Gannett, Jeff. Fate of Mary Ellen Van Twerp
Gannett, Jeff. Where's the baby?
George, Charles. Entertaining sister's beaux
George, Charles. It might happen
George, Charles. Proposal
George, Charles. So you won't talk
Kaser, A. L. Historical hystericals
Kaser, A. L. Landing of Columbus
Kaser, A. L. Man versus dog
Kaser, A. L. School days
Kaser, A. L. Their first play
Kaser, A. L. There's going to be a wedding
Kaser, A. L. What a classroom!
Kaser, A. L. Ye old time vaudeville
Phelps, Franklin. Henry the model husband
Phelps, Franklin. King's toemaine
Phelps, Franklin. Sudden riches
Provence, Jean. Not for credit
Royce, Bob. Bill the matchmaker
Steele, Sidney. First rehearsal
Steele, Sidney. Have a good time
Steele, Sidney. It's her, or the car
Steele, Sidney. Liar's club
Steele, Sidney. Mental marvel
    Also Blackouts, Talking acts, Pantomimes, Monologues, Stunts,
    Games.

Brings, L. M. ed. One-act dramas & contest plays. Minneapolis, Denison,
1962.

Ramsey, Helen. Room upstairs
Finch, Robert. Old Grad
Hunter, S. McK. Sod
Provence, Jean. Plucked peacocks
George, Charles. Evening star
McMahon, Luella E. First Mrs. Paris
Duthie, Hermine. Wheat fire

Fletcher, Winifred B. White tablecloth
Brome, Robert. Winter sunset
Pitner, Monty. Decision
Howe, Grace P. Grandma
Gatlin, Dana. Turning point
Mannix, Helen W. We Brents pay our debts

Brings, L. M. comp. Rehearsal-less skits & plays. Minneapolis, Denison, 1963.
Sheldon, G. E. Old village school
Sheldon, G. E. Little Red Riding Hood
Sheldon, G. E. Three modern bears
Sheldon, G. E. In the land of Schmozz
Sheldon, G. E. Inconsequential journeys
Sheldon, G. E. Your screen test
Sheldon, G. E. Musical answers
Sheldon, G. E. Nobody knows
Sheldon, G. E. The ham that am
Sheldon, G. E. Crime Club
Sheldon, G. E. Whole Famdamily
Sheldon, G. E. Fatal scream
Sheldon, G. E. At home with the range
Sheldon, G. E. Missing false teeth
Sheldon, G. E. Still in the night
Huber, L. J. Reversal in rehearsal
Huber, L. J. Cards on the table
Huber, L. J. Man of many miens
Huber, L. J. School daze minstrels
Huber, L. J. Waiter who waited
Huber, L. J. Outcome of income
Huber, L. J. It's a silly game
Huber, L. J. Defective detective
Huber, L. J. All who enter
Huber, L. J. Newspaper nightmare
Huber, L. J. Do I bother you?
Huber, L. J. Mills that grind
Huber, L. J. Let's modernize
Huber, L. J. Order in the court
Drummond, Richard. First rehearsal
Drummond, Richard. What a game! What a game!
Drummond, Richard. Prof. Cuckoo, crystal gazer
Drummond, Richard. Flowers & weeds
Drummond, Richard. True story of Capt. John Smith
Drummond, Richard. At the corner drug store
Drummond, Richard. Harmony a la hobo
Drummond, Richard. District school at Carrot Corners
Drummond, Richard. Bill, the matchmaker
Drummond, Richard. Substitute bride
Drummond, Richard. What a mess
Drummond, Richard. Eye-opener
Drummond, Richard. Henry, the model husband

Drummond, Richard. High pressure
Stahl, Le Roy. Pocahontas
Stahl, Le Roy. Prince & the Sleeping Beauty
Stahl, Le Roy. With General Wow in darkest Africa
Stahl, Le Roy. One hundred & forty four davenports
Stahl, Le Roy. Mail order dragon

Brown, Regina. A play for your house. N. Y. Obolensky, 1962.
Little Women
Through the looking glass
Racketty-packetty house
Little Princess
Adventure of Tom Sawyer

Browne, E. M. ed. 21 medieval mystery & morality plays. N. Y. Meridian, 1958.
Creation of man (York)
Creation of the heavenly beings, the fall of Lucifer (York)
Garden of Eden (York)
Fall of man (York)
Noah's flood (Chester)
Sacrifice of Isaac (Brome)
David takes the shoots to Jerusalem (Cornish)
Parliament of heaven; the annunciation & Conception (Hegge)
Birth of Christ (York)
Play of the shepherds (Wakefield)
Herod & the Kings (Coventry)
Temptation of Christ (York)
Woman taken in adultery (Hegge)
Palm Sunday (York)
Second trial before pilate: the scourging and condemnation (York)
Crucifixion (York)
Harrowing of hell (York)
Three Maries (Cornish)
Ascension (York)
Last judgment (York)
Everyman (Morality)

Burack, A. S. ed. Four-star palys for boys. Bost. Plays, 1957.
Sayre, G. W. Final edition
Clark, B. H. Fires of Valley Forge
Shore, Maxime. Catastrophe Clarence
Suerken, E. H. John Crowe's legacy
Burlingame, Cora. Yellow fever
Miller, Helen L. Jiminy Cinders
Colson, J. G. Robin Hood in Sherwood forest
Harper, J. M. First cat on Mars
Colson, J. G. Top of the bill
Nicholson, Mary A. Crying clown
Holmes, Ruth V. King John & the Abbot of Canterbury
Bennett, Rowena. Runaway pirate

Werner, Sally. Home Sweet Home
Molloy, Lida L. Fortune of Merry legs & tawny whiskers.

Burack, A. S. ed. Prize contest plays for young people. Boston Plays, 1962.
Allred, Pearl. Orchids for Margaret
Miller, Helen L. N for nuisance
Nicholson, Jessie. Mind over matter
Murdock, Marion L. The cuckoo
Miller, Marion L. Cry witch
Downing, Robert. Sticks & stones
Hark, Mildred. Minority of millions
Alderman, Elinor R. Anyone for the moon?
Sanders, J. A. Ten-penny tragedy
Garver, Juliet. Nerve of Napoleon
Allred, Joan. Society page
Downing, Robert. Jimmy six
Martens, Anne C. Runaway
Nolan, P. T. Straw boy

Burack, A. S. comp. Treasury of holiday plays for teen-agers. Boston, Plays, 1963.
Garver, Juliet. Father of the year
DuBois, Graham. With malice toward none
Callaman, Cecelia C. Cupid & Co.
Garver, Juliet. Happy Valentine Day
Dias, E. J. General Gage's chowder
Wolman, Diana. Imaginary trial of George Washington
Campbell, Josephine E. St. Patrick's eve
Pendleton, Edrie. Hats & rabbits
Miller, Helen L. Mother's hidden talent
Downing, Robert. Second Sunday in May
Martens, Anne C. Nor long remember
Fisher, Helen L. Broomstick beauty
Murray, John. Old ghosts at home
Hark, Mildred. Know the truth
Hark, Mildred. Case for books
Du Bois, Graham. Everyday is Thanksgiving Day
Hark, Mildred. Thanksgiving postscript
Phillips, Marguerite K. Man behind the book
Olfson, Lewy. Christmas coast to coast
Du Bois, Graham. Song in the night
Miller, Helen L. Christmas cowboy
Pendleton, Edrie. 'Twas the night before Christmas

C

Carlson, Bernice W. The right play for you. N. Y. Abingdon, 1960.
A traitor's reward
Near mutiny on the Santa Maria
Altogether! Heave!

Jim Bridger & his eight-hour echo
For soldiers everywhere
    Also much valuable material

Carroll, P. V. Irish stories & plays. N. Y. Devin-Adair, 1958.
The conspirators
Beauty is fled
Interlude
    Also 8 short stories, and a long play.

Carver, C. H. & others. America today. Englewood Cliffs, N. J. Prentice, 1959.
Mindel, Joseph B. B. Franklin, American
Rose, Reginald. Almanac of liberty
Wilder, Thornton. Happy journey to Trenton & Camden
Medcraft, Russell. First dress-suit
    Also much valuable material.

Carver, C. H. & others. They found adventure. Englewood Cliffs, Prentice, 1960.
Mosel, Tad. Jinxed
O'Neil, Eugene. In the zone
Vidal, Gore. Visit to a small planet
    Much additional valuable material.

Carver, C. H. & others. Youth & the future.
Mosel, Tad. Five dollar bill
Ludwig, William. "Interruptions, interruptions"
Gilsdorf, Frederick. Ghost of Benjamin Sweet
    Also much valuable material.

Casey, Bernice M. Good things for Mother's Day. Minneapolis, Denison, 1960.
The coach
All the world loves a mother
It's tough on mother
Lucky piece for Mom
Making mother over
Mothering Miss Mittie
Violets for Mother's Day
Your Mom & my Mom

Casey, F. J. Staging the Bible. Westminister, Maryland, Newman, 1962.
Book of Job
The family
The good & the evil
Promised Messiah
Sermon on the mount
Bread of life
Week before his death
Passion & death of Jesus Christ

Peter & the early church
I, Paul—prisoner
Charity in the Epistle of James & John
Creation sings the glory of God

Cerf, Bennett & Cartwell, V. H. 24 favorite one-act plays. N. Y. Doubleday, 1958.

Miller, Arthur. Memory of two Mondays
Rattingan, Terence. Browning version
Williams, Tennessee. 27 wagon loads of cotton
Fletcher, Lucille. Sorry, wrong number
Inge, William. Glory in the flower
Coward, Noel. Hands across the sea
Benet, S. V. Devil & Daniel Webster
Wilder, Thornton. Happy journey
Parker, Dorothy. Here we are
Connelly, Marc. Traveler
Kaufman, G. S. Still alarm
O'Neil, Eugene. Moon of the Caribbees
Down, Oliphant. Maker of dreams
Kelly, George. Flattering word
Lardner, Ring. Tridget of Greva
Giraudoux, Jean. Apollo of Bellac
Glaspel, Susan. Trifles
Milne, A. A. Ugly duckling
Dunsany, Lord. Jest of Hahalaba
Synge, J. M. In the shadow of the glen
Yeats, W. B. Cathleen ni Houlihan
Chekhov, Anton. Marriage proposal
Gregory, Lady. Spreading the news
Wilde, Oscar. Florintine tragedy

Citron, S. J. ed. Dramatics the year round. N. Y. United Synagogue
Com'n. 1956.

Zweig, Esther S. Holiday minstrels
Citron, S. J. If not even higher
Podolyn, J. C. Going to a party
Zion, Deborah. To the new world
Citron, S. J. 23 & Reyna
Citron, S. J. Jug of oil
Hyman, Frieda C. Little candle that wouldn't
Becker, C. S. Night before Hanukah
Solis-Cohen, Emily. Magic top
Kessler, Harry. Modern Modin
Levinger, Elma E. Unlighted Menorah
Kabakoff, Dorothy. Comrades all
Citron, S. J. Be not afraid
Herman, M. J. Brother Sam
Citron, S. J. Four Chaplains
Wishengrad, Morton. My cousin Avigdor
Citron, S. J. Eliezer Ben Yehudah

Grossman, S. S. Vote for Haman
Wishengrad, Morton. Song for Queen Esther
Garvey, Robert. Passover story
Citron, S. J. The magician
Citron, S. J. Jerusalem
Mittleman. Shavot day dream
Citron, S. J. Herzl comes home
Learsi, Rufus. To the young, a vision
Learsi, Rufus. Bar Giora
Segal, Sadie W. Hillel the student
Franklin, Harold. Freedom Hall
Aronin, Ben. Great women of Israel
Kaplin, L. L. We pledge allegiance

Clapp, E. R. & others. College Quad. N. Y. Dryden, 1956.
Joad, C. E. M. That no one book is better than another
Dryer, B. V. Typhus
   Also much more material.

Clark, B. H. ed. World drama. N. Y. Dover, n.d.
Aeschylus. Prometheus bound
Sophocles. Antigone
Aristophanes. The clouds
Euripides. Alcestis
Plautus. The captives
Semi. Nakamitsu
Sachs. Wandering scholar from Paradise
Marlow. Tragic history of Dr. Faustis
Terence. Phormio
———— Adam
———— Second Shepherd's play
———— Wise virgins & the foolish virgins
———— Farce of the worthy Master Pierre Patelin
———— Play of St. George
———— Everyman
   Also many full length plays.

Clark, B. H. ed. World drama. 2. N. Y. Dover, n.d.
Beolco, Angelo. Bilora
Scala, Fliminiio. The portrait
Cervantes. Cave of Salamanca
   Also many full length plays.

Cook, Luella B. & others. People in literature. N. Y. Harcourt, 1957.
Ferber, Edna. The eldest
Wilder, Thornton. Happy journey
Lampell, Millard. Lonesome train
   Also much other material.

Coward, Noel. Collected plays of Noel Coward. Olay Parade Vol. 4. London, Heinamann, 1954.
We are dancing

Astonished heart
Red peppers
Hands across the sea
Fumed oak
Shadow play
Ways & means
Still life
Family album
   Also two longer plays.

D

Dale, Chalmers, ed. In the presence of death. St. Louis, Bethany, 1964.

Hamilton, William. Till death do us part
Gilbert, Craig. End of the story
Chodobov, Stephan. Journal of Vera Grey
Hamilton, William. Room for death

Decker, R. G. ed. N. Y. Oxford, 1959.

Van Druten, J. I remember mama
Laidlaw, George. Command decision
Osborne Paul. Madame Curie
Rose, Reginald. Almanac of liberty
Valency, Maurice. Second stranger
Cotton, Helen. Hand-me-down
Corwin, Norman. Ann Rutledge

Dias, E. J. One-act plays for teen-agers. Boston Plays, 1961.

Landslide for Shakespeare
Printer's devil
Hold back the Redskins
Bow-wow blues
Beatnick & the Bard
Cleanest town in the West
Treasure at Bentley Inn
Gift of Laughter
Video Christmas
Christmas spirit
Dear Lollie
Cast up by the sea
Little man who wasn't there
The mantle
Madison Ave., merry-go-round

Downer, A. S. comp. Art of the play. N. Y. Holt, 1955.

Aeschylus. Prometheus bound
O'Neil, Eugene. Emperor Jones
Sophocles. Oedipus Rex
   Also six longer plays

Dramatist Play Service. 14 East 38th. St. N. Y. Separates.

Durrell, Donald & Crossley, Alice. comp. 30 plays for classroom reading.
Boston, Plays, 1957.
Lesser, Eleanor. Five brothers
Howard, Helen L. Ben Franklin, peace-maker
Barr, June. Lion & the mouse
Reines B. J. Turncoat
Howard, Helen L. Thankful indeed
Holmes, Ruth V. In the days of King Alfred
Asbrand, Karin. Adalamina's pearl
Newman, Deborah. Magic goose
Felsbein, Jerry. Ali Baba & the 40 thieves
Worcester, Natalia S. Mad tea party
Simonds, Natalie. Hansel & Gretel
McLellan, Esther. Return of the Nina
Haggy, Loleta. Fire in a paper
Faux, D. Littlest month
Colbo, Ella S. Heroine of Wren
McLellan, Esther. Needle fights for freedom
St. Clair, Robert. Miss Muffet's wish
Howard, Helen L. What he deserves
Bennett, Rowena. Runaway pirate
McMeekin, I. Runaway Balloon
Cooper, Esther. Greta & the Prince
McLellan, Esther. Small shoes & small tulips
Urban, Catherine. Who started the fire
Williams, G. M. Kettle of brains
King, Walter. Snow White
Fisher, Aileen. One-ring circus
Hark, Mildred. House is haunted
Ickles, Lyda M. Kitty Hawk
Fisher, Aileen. King's toothache
Fisher, Aileen. Invasion from the Stratosphere

E

Edades, Jean. ed. More short plays of the Philippines. Manila, Benipayo,
1957.
Rojo, J. At stake
Buenafe, M. Resignation
Buenafe, M. Return of the warrior
Quiambao, E. A. The papers
Carino, Jose. Brown Man's burden
Bayot, A. O. Finishing touches
Medina, A. E. Technique is the thing
Sican, F. Cowards die a thousand deaths
Florentino, A. S. World is an apple
Drummond, R. R. Three of them
Taylor, Isabel. The strike

Bautista, P. F. Prelude to glory
Pascual, I. V. R. Toots
Tabunar, E. Angry sea
Florentino, A. S. Cadaver
    Also longer play.

Edades, Jean, ed. Short plays of the Philippines. Manila, Benipayo, 1958.
Villa, Lela. Educating Josefina
Rodrigo, F. Sa pula, sa puti
Mack, Rachel. Augustina of the light heart
Castro, N. H. At the turn of the road
Estagle, Felicina. Awakening
Palarca, Julia. Other tomorrows
Mack, Rachel. Cristina goes by with goats
Mijares, J. M. Princess is sorry
Alfiler, Mercedes. Pinno goes to Hollywood
Nalasco, D. Help wanted
Nalasco, D. Ranger takes a wife
Wong, Benjamin. Best way to die
Tan, Vidal. Souls in torment
Rojo, I. Living dead man
Sicum, G. D. Mir-I-Nisa
Edades, Jean. Magic fruit
Taylor, Isabel. Efficient expert
    Also longer play.

Emmons, Delia G. Northwest history in action. Minneapolis, Denison, 1960.
Toehold for the U.S.A.
Out to win
John Jewitt, the slave
Astor's bid for empire
Answering the call
Joint occupation, joint celebration
Who's for the divide?
Costly gold hunt
Through Natches Pass
Territory is born
Statehood for Washington
    Also a pageant.

Emurian, E. K. Ten new plays for church & school. Natick, Mass., Wilde, 1959.
Inasmuch
Three skits for Christmas
Famous families
Charles Wesley
I'll take you home again, Kathleen
Uncle Sam
Stewards of the soul

Living dramatization of the Beatitudes
The first breakfast
   Also one longer play

Estes, Susan. In quest of power. Nashville, Broadman, 1954.
Through prayer
Through the Holy Spirit
Through obedience
Through Faith
Through decision
Through courage
Through humility
Through witnessing
Through divine guidance
Through wisdom
Through dedication
Through prophecy

Everard, Elizabeth, ed. Ten one- act plays for women. London, Harrap. 1958.
Morris, T. B. Apple-pie order
Morris, T. B. Check to the Queen
Ratcliff, Nora. Daughters of invention
Bolton, Mada G. Everybody comes to Mabel
Bolton, Mada G. Her affairs in order
Godefroy, Vincent. Intermezzo
Maule, Wendy St. J. Ladies-in-waiting
Bannister, Winifred. No stars for Henry
Matheson, Mary F. Phantom ship
Russell, Eileen. Two women

F

Feigenbraum, L. A. ed. Radio & television plays. N. Y. Globe, 1956.
Fletcher, Lucile. Sorry, wrong number
Harmon, D. P. Melody man
Obler, Arch. The word
Tunick, James. She walks in beauty
Latham, John. One in twelve
Serling, Rod. U F O
Chevigny, Hector. Daniel Webster

Felheim, Marvin. Plays, theory & criticism. N. Y. Harcourt, 1962.
Chekhov, Anton. A wedding
Shaw, G. B. Man of destiny
Fry, Christopher. Phoenix too often
   Also long plays, and other valuable material.

Fenenga, J. & others. Pilot series in literature. Book 1. Michigan, Grand Rapids, 1957.
Parsons, Margaret. Sailing west to find the east

Cameron, Irene. By the dawn's early light
Also much valuable material.

Fenner, Phyllis & Hughes, Avah. Entrances & exits. N. Y. Dodd, 1960.
Holmes, Ruth V. King John & the Abbot of Canterbury
Field, Rachel. Polly Patchwork
Pyle, Mary T. Not on the menu
Totheroh, Dan. Stolen Prince
Gow, Ronald. Under the skull & bones
Jagendorf, M. Merry Tyll
Goldsmith, Sophie L. How boots befooled the King
Goldsmith, Sophie L. Staff & the fiddle
Fisher, Aileen. Merry Christmas elf
Wright, Lula. Mr. Popper's penguins
Barnes, Emily A. Sokar & the crocodile
Barnes, Emily A. Magic fishbone
Klein, Muriel W. Ali Baba & the 40 thieves
Lewis, Mary R. Dick Whittington

Fisher, Aileen. Christmas plays & programs. Boston, Plays, 1960.
A tree to trim
Inn at Bethlehem
Mr. Scrooge finds Christmas
What happened in Toyland
Christmas in court
Calling all Christmases
On such a night
Nine cheers for Christmas
Sing the song of Christmas
Setting Santa Claus straight
Mother Goose's party
Christmas tablecloth
Standing up to Santa Claus
What's for Christmas
Christmas quarantine
Shoes & stockings & Solomon
Say it with rhymes
Week before Christmas
Stable at midnight
Gift of St. Nick
Something in the air
Up a Christmas tree
Christmas spelldown
Trimming the tree
Also recitations, poems, songs & games

Fisher, Aileen & Rabe, Olive. Patriotic plays & programs. Boston, Plays 1956.
What's a patriot
Sing, America, sing
Champions of democracy

Dish of green peas
Flag of freedom
May the best man win
Haym Solomon's battle
Apostle of freedom
Not for sale
Star for Old Glory
Shipmates
Stage set for Veterans' Day
Honest Abe Lincoln
When freedom was news
Anonymous letter
Johnny on the spot
Immigrants all, Americans all
Rockets to freedom
Our great Declaration
Bringing up father
Wheels within wheels
Pledge to the flag
Long may it wave
Ask Mr. Jefferson
Yankee Doodle Dandy
Johnny Appleseed's vision
"Molly Pitcher"
    Also Group reading, Spelldowns, recitations

Fisher, Aileen. Plays about our nation's songs. Boston Plays, 1962.

Sing, America, sing
Sing the songs of freedom
Sing the songs of pioneers
Sing the songs of Thanksgiving
Sing the songs of Christmas
Sing the songs of Lincoln
Sing the songs of Springtime
Sing the songs of Travel
Sing the songs of Cowboys
Sing the songs of Growing

Fisher, Aileen & Rabe, Olive. U.N. plays & programs. Boston, Plays, 1965.

Thanks a million
All the world round
Cavalcade of human rights
Alice in Puzzleland
Best bargain in the world
Invasion from the stratosphere
Let there be bread
Turning the tables
Accident of birth
Nickel & a dime
What happened in Egypt

Of gods & men
Get-together dinner
Skills to share
Story of a well
Fresco for Unesco
All in the U.N.
Getting in line
Empty bowls

Florentino, A. S. Outstanding Filipino short plays. Manila, Filipinana, 1961.

Recto, C. M. Shadow & solitude
Montano, S. Sabina
Guerrero, W. M. Three rats
Bayot, A. O. Among the faithless
Florentino, A. S. The dancers
Flores, J. T. Scent of fear
Molledo, W. D. Goodbye my gentle
Peralta, J. T. Summer funeral

Free Company Presents. Collection of plays about the meaning of America. N. Y. Dodd, 1941.

Saroyan, William. People with light coming out of them
Connelly, Marc. Mole on Lincoln's cheek
Boyd, James. One more free man
Sherwood, R. E. American crusader
Benet, S. V. Freedom's a hard-bought thing
Welles, Orson. His honor, the mayor
Green, Paul. Start in life
MacLeish, Archibald. States talking
Anderson, Maxwell. Miracle of the Danube
Anderson, Maxwell. Above suspicion

Fry, Christopher. Three plays. N. Y. Oxford, 1961.

Thor with angels
A sleep of prisoners
    Also longer play.

G

Graham, C. B. comp. English freshman Program. Chicago, Scott Foresman, 1960.

Sophocles. Oedipus the King
O'Neil, Eugene. Bound east for Cardiff
    Also two long plays and other valuable material.

Green, Paul. Five plays of the South. N. Y. Hill & Wang, 1960.

Hymn to the rising sun
White dresses
In Abraham's bosom
    Also two long plays.

Guder, Eileen L. What happened after . . . Los Angeles, Cowman, 1962.
What child is this?
Status seeker
Man with the question
Young man of means
Women at the well
Give us this day
Women in the kitchen
This firebrand
Unwelcome vision
All in a day's work

Gunn, John, ed. The seeking years. St. Louis, Bethany, 1959.
Rodman, Howard. Faith healer
Kellerman, Benjamin. No man is an island
Rodman, Howard. Thing of beauty
Roskan, Clair. The puzzle
Roskan, Clair. Plenty of rein
Rodman, Howard. Snow drifting

H

Halverson, Marion. Religious drama. No. I. N. Y. Meridian, 1957.
Auden, W. H. For the time being
Lawrence, D. H. David
Sayers, Dorothy. Zeal of the house
Schevill, James. Bloody tenet
    Also a longer play.

Halverson, Marion. ed. Religious drama. No. 3. N. Y. Living Age, 1959.
Broughton, James. Last word
Williams, James. House by the stable
Williams, James. Grab & grace
Cummings, E. E. Santa Claus
Phelps, Luon. Gospel witch
Mankowitz, Wolf. It should happen to a dog
Lagerkvist, Par. Let man live
    Also a longer play.

Hark, Mildred & McQueen, Noel. Special plays for special days. Boston, Plays, 1960.
Abe Lincoln & little Joe
Kindly heart
Let George do it
Echo of '76
Saint Patrick
Magic egg
Mother Earth's new dress
Forest fantasy
We want mother
Mother's admirers

Forward march
Stars & stripes
Three V's
Glory he deserves
Under the harvest moon
Book magic
Bunch of keys
Knight for safety
Thanksgiving with Uncle Sam
Day of thanks
What, no Santa Claus!
Christmas eve letter
Boy with a future
A chance to do better

Hark, Mildred & McQueen, Noel. Teen-age plays for all occasions, Boston, Plays, 1957.

Homecoming
Ode to Spring
Cabana blues
Spring daze
G for Gettysburg
Heart trouble
To my Valentine
Bake a cherry pie
First in peace
Mother's V.I.P.'s
Mom's perfect day
Portrait of an American
Who's old-fashioned?
Halloween luck
Vote for your hero
Books are bridges
Aladdin steps out
If we could only cook
What, no venison?
Reindeer on the roof
Christmas recaptured
All aboard for Christmas

Havinghurst, Walter & others. Selections, N. Y. Dryden, 1955.

Sophocles. Antigone
Synge, J. M. Riders to the sea
Williams, Tennessee. Glass menagerie
  Also longer play and other material.

Hayes, Richard, comp. Port Royal & other plays. N. Y. Hill & Wang, 1962.

Montherlaut, Henry de. Port Royal
Copeau, Jaques. Little poor man
  Also two longer plays.

Holbrook, David, comp. Thieves & angels. London, Cambridge Uni. 1962.
Bird-catcher in hell
Second shepherd's play of the nativity
Abraham & Isaac
Bunyan. Pilgrim's progress
Death in the tree
Falstaff at Gadshill
Punch & Judy
Also longer play, and other material.

Hook, J. N. & others. Literature of adventure. Boston, Ginn, 1957.
Nurnberg, Maxwell. American names
Niggle, Josephina. This bull ate nutmeg
Also much additional material.

Hopper, V. F. & Lahey, G. B. ed. Medieval mystery plays N. Y. Barron's
Educational series, 1962.
Abraham & Isaac
Noah's flood
Castle of perseverance
Second shepherd's play
Johan, Johan
The four pp.

Housman, Laurance, Gracious Majesty. N. Y. Scribner, 1957.
A heavy change
The bell
Order of precedence
Popular voice
Extremes meet
Domestic difference
Visit to Birmingham
Ruling powers
Superlative relative
Recollections
This is the heir
Life in the Highlands

Howard, Vernon, comp. Short plays from the great classics. London,
Sterling, 1960.
Treasure of Monte Cristo
Oliver Twist asks for more
Johnny Appleseed in danger
Sir Galahad & the maidens
Happy holidays for Little Women
David & Goliath
Return of Rip Van Winkle
Strange tale of King Midas
Around the world—by way of America
Gulliver wins his freedom

Swiss Family Robinson—rescued
Don Quixote saves the day

Huber, L. J. Humorous acts for stunt programs. Minneapolis, Denison, 1963.
Fight to a finish
Baby hands
Bent fender
By your hand
Competition
Use the book
Clean-hands
I'm not here
Stay awake
Tell no tales
Call me Dear
Days gone by
In union
Don't cry, baby
Medicine man
Innocent bystander
Sound effects man
Baby sitter
Male model
Hurry Doctor
Some fun, son
Let's pretend
Property man
Be careful, judge
Kill the Ump
Fountain of youth
Love's labor
Free samples
Also vaudeville skits.

Huberman, Edward & Raymo, R. R. Angles of vision. Boston Houghton, 1962.
Wedekind, The tenor
Also two long plays and other material.

I

Inge, William. Summer brave & eleven short plays. N. Y. Random, 1962.
To bobolink, for her spirit
People in the wind
Social event
Boy in the basement
Tiny closet
Memory of summer
Bus Riley's back in town
Rainy afternoon

The wall
An incident at Standish Arms
   Also longer play

Iverson, W. J. & McCarthy, Agnes L. Prose & poetry journeys. 5th. ed. Syracuse N. Y. Singer, 1957.

Gilsdorf, Paulina. Ghost of Benjamin Sweet
Covington, W. P. Shirttail boy
   And much additional material.

J

Jagendorf, Moritz, ed. 20 non-royalty one-act ghost plays. N. Y. Greenberg, 1946.

Taylor, M. A. Dilly Dehaunting Agency
Greene, C. G. Your rooms are ready
Relonde, Maurice. Happy ending of a gruesome ghost
Courtney, Pauline. Uncle Petey
Dustmann, Walter. Indignant ghost
Stoler, S. A. Ghost by request
Haunterton, N. Headless horseman
Welff, Erid. Ghost of Caesar's hair
West, Margaret K. Madame Dode
Defer, Marion. Three squeals for freedom
Bella, M. Dark walkers
Morawsky, Marie. Vacant room
Simon, Irving. Ghost a la mode
Very, Alice. Highland lad
Rider, Francis. Two ghosts are better than one
Lehman, Gene. Ghost of laughing Dan
Harmer, Mabel. Ghosts on strike
Hocking, Nancy M. Good ghosts
Cox, W. E. Return of Michael Conley
Boretz, Alvin. Camp ghost

John, Gwen. Plays. London, Duckworth, n.d.

Outlaws
Sealing the compact
Edge o'dark
Case of Teresa
In the Rector's study

Johnson, Crane. Over sixty. San Francisco, International Theatre, 1953.

George Washington's chair
Astonishing Mrs. O'Shaugnessy
The proposal
The rockers

Johnson, Denis. The old lady says 'no' & other plays. Boston, Atlantic, 1961.

The old lady says "no"

Fourth for bridge
Dreaming dust
  Also longer plays.

K

Kamerman, Sylvia E. ed. Blue-ribbon plays for graduation. Boston, Plays, 1957.
Marcus, I. H. To you the torch
Hark, Mildred. The place to begin
Fisher, Aileen. Sing, America, sing
Downing, Robert. Sticks & stones
Flaten, Mary. Testing ground for democracy
Paradis, Marjory B. Midge rings the bell
Fisher, Aileen. Cavalcade of human rights
Hackett, Walter. Outgoing tide
Miller, Helen L. New shoes
Orme, Frank. Graduation present

Kamerman, Sylvia E. ed. Treasury of Christmas plays. Boston, Plays, 1958.
Hark, Mildred. Merry Christmas, Crawfords!
Du Bois, Graham. Room for the King
Miller, Louise H. Monsieur Santa Claus
Dias, E. J. Christmas spirit
Larson, Edith. Christmas bug
Du Bois, Graham. Humblest place
Morley, Olive J. Little women
Thurston, Muriel B. Room for Mary
Paradis, Marjorie B. None but the fair
Phillips, M. R. Violets for Christmas
Miller, Helen L. Season's greetings
Waite, Helen E. Master of the strait
Morley, Olive J. O Little town of Bethlehem
Fisher, Aileen. Sing the songs of Christmas
Nicholson, Jessie. Holiday for Santa
Peterson, Mary N. Adobe Christmas
Runnette, Helen V. Touchstone
Capell, Loretta C. First Christmas tree
Leuser, Eleanor D. Christmas sampler
Runnette, Helen V. The way
Duvall, Lucile M. Chosen one
Fisher, Aileen. Nine cheers for Christmas
Wright, Doris G. Twelve days of Christmas
Leuser, Eleanor D. Legend of the Christmas rose
Bennett, Rowena. Granny Goodman's Christmas
Spanner, Claribel. Twinkle
Barr, June. White Christmas
Howard, Helen L. Candles for Christmas
Hark, Mildred. Merry Christmas customs

Fuente Sagrada
The sniper
All roads lead to Rome

L

Long, W. I. Twelve half-hours with Winthrop Theatre. Rock, So. Carolina, Winthrop College, 1959.
Federspiel, Jo Ann, D. Behold the body
Ouzts, Joyce D. Happy pagan
Nappier, Patricia. Just a matter of timing
Nichols, Jane. 'Twas such a night
Sanders, Betty LeN. What's cookin'
Elam, Rebecca C. Duchess of Dogwood
Horne, Kay A. This dark world & wide lane
Quinn, Carolyn. For want of character
McLaughlin, Miriam. Mind's construction
Ouzts, Joyce D. Happy pagan
Nappier, Patricia. And there was light
Manning, Sally. As silent as the ocean

M

Macneice, Louis. Mad island & the administrator. London, Faber, 1964.
Mad island
Administrator

Mayorga, Margaret. ed. Best short plays of 1955-1956. Boston, Beacon, 1956.
Berrini, Alberto. Once a thief
Mac Leish, Archibald. This music crept by me upon the waters
Williams, Tennessee. Something unspoken
Zeigler, Henry. The High School
Purkey, Ruth A. Hangs over thy head
Rose, Reginald. Dime
Walsh, Norman. Let there be farce
Gurney, A. R. J. Three people
Seiger, M. L. Blue concerto
    Also one longer play.

Mayorga, Margaret. ed. Best short plays of 1957-1958. Boston, Beacon, 1958.
Gurney, A. R. J. Turn of the century
Kleinsinger, George. Archie & Mehitabel
Welch, Rae. Let's get out of here
Stockton, R. F. A fabulous tale
Snyder, W. H. The departing
Young, Stanley. Sound of apples
Scholl, Ralph. Golden axe

Devany, E. M. Red & yellow ark
Makowsky, Lucile. The new world
  And a two act television play.

Mayorga, Margaret, ed. Best short plays of 1958-1959. Boston, Beacon, 1959.

Devany, E. H. The cow-catcher on the caboose
Inge, William. Tiny closet
Woskoff, Vera. Castle in the village
Richards, Stanley. Gin & bitterness
Senior, Edward. The hunted
Zuckerman, A. J. Blobo's boy
Conkle, E. P. Heaven is a long time to wait
Proverman, Helen. Easy money
Potter, D. S. Touch of marble
Procunier, E. R. Two sides of darkness

Mayorga, Margaret, ed. Best short plays of 1959-1960. Boston, Beacon, 1960.

Seiler, Conrad. Nude washing dishes
Perl, Arnold. Tevya & the first daughter
Albee, Edward. Sandbox
Perry, Marjean. Two's company
Goldman, Paul. Mermaid Avenue is the world
States, B. O. Tall grass
Roepke, Gabriela. White butterfly
Stein, Howard. Sight for sore thoughts
Aguirre, Isadora. Express for Santiago
Dace, Wallace. We commit this body

Mayorga, Margaret, ed. Best short plays of 1960-1961. Boston, Beacon, 1962.

Campbell, J. G. Summit conference
Brophy, Edmund. Nothin' to nothin'
Weber, W. L. Miracle of the boar
Greene, R. A. Eliza & the lexicon
Else, George. Joey
Apstein, Theodore. Wetback run
Carlson, Julia B. The monster
Holland, Norman. Wages of sin
Purley, Ruth A. Let go the dream
Malcolm, Ian. This gentlemen, is justice

Malcolmson, Anne, ed. Miracle plays. Boston, Houghton, 1959.

Abraham & Isaac
Noah's flood
Shepherd's play
Nativity
Herod & the Magi
Statue of St. Nicholas
St. Nicholas & the three scholars

Maugham, W. S. Encore. N. Y. Doubleday, 1952.

Ant & the grasshopper
Winter cruise
Gigolo & Gigolet
    Also stories & longer plays.

Mc

McCaslin, Nellie. Pioneers in petticoats. Evanston, Row Peterson, 1960.

Cold face—warm heart
Bluebonnets
Mercy in Moccasins
Legend of Minna Lamovrie
Miracle of the Christmas city
Brave new banner
Daring darling Dolly
Too many cooks
Prelude to fame
Leading lady
Lost horizon
Angel of the battlefield
Straight shooter

McCaslin, Nellie. Tall tales & tall men. Philadelphia, Macrae, 1956.

Bell witch of Tennessee
John Henry
With sunrise in his pocket
Tall Bill & his big ideas
Apples in the wilderness
Yankee peddler
Seafaring giant
He traveled the world
Saint Nicholas of Amsterdam
Gift of corn
Star that never moves

McCoy, P. S. Just for variety. Evanston, Row Peterson, 1958.

High pressure
Curtain capers
Voice from nowhere
Date with Patsy
Petal in the dust
For women only

McCoy, P. S. Modern comedies for teen-agers. Boston, Plays, 1962.

You don't belong to me
Miss Fixit
Instructions for Gary
Farewell to Calvin
No treat for Gilbert
She's not talking

Greetings from the Fultons
Hold your hat
Luncheon for three
Keep it under cover
Take care, Anne
Johnny nightmare
Briefly speaking
Cicero the Great
Two for the show
Word of honor
You'd never think it
Double talk

McCrea, Lillian. Puppets & puppet plays. London, Oxford, 1952.

Betty & her friends
Betty's surprise
Betty's birthday
Rainy day
Father Christmas
Mummy's secret
Dog for Betty
Mother Hen
Three bears
Little Red Riding Hood
David's rabbits
Story of Christmas

McKellar, H. D. ed. Beyond the footlights. Toronto, Macmillan, 1963.

Williams, Norman. Protest
Daviot, Gordon. Remember Caesar
Niggli, Josephina. Ring for General Macias
Benet, S. V. A child is born
Hill, Kay. Three to get married
Hardy, Thomas. Three wayfarers
Procunier, Edwin. Two sides of darkness
Tolstoi, Leo. What men live by

Miksch, W. F. Teen-age comedies. Minneapolis, Denison, 1962.

Day of adventure
Help wanted—badly
Afternoon at Central station
Sweater girls
Oh, waitress!
Holiday home coming
Science is wonderful
Anybody's gift
It's no picnic
Keep smiling
I want a policeman
Dates are big business
How to study

Out in the rain again
Sound punctuation
Playful bus
Hollywood play
Take-off
Soloist
We deliver most anywhere
Daylight saving
Expanding trade
Some interference!
Big hunt
Watch the birdie
Helping hand
First aid without aiding
Art alliance
Is thrift a virtue?
Dancing lesson
Emergency Doctor
Back seat pilot
House guest
Subscribe now
Sitting tonight
End of the line
Idol worshipers
Entertainment committee
Blind date
Craftsman
Star dust
Life is so dull
Evening bells
Camp Crowhill, here we come
Affair in the park
Swank night

Miller, Helen L. Easy plays for boys & girls. Boston, Plays, 1963.

Little nut tree
Bandit Ben rides again
Sourdough Sally
Aloha, mother
So long at the fair
Glass slipper
Mouse that soared
Smokey wins his star
Meet Mr. Muffy
Admiral's nightmare
Which way to Halloween?
Runaway unicorn
Parrot & the pirates
A B C's Thanksgiving
Bartholomew's joyful noise
Runaway toys

Squeaknibble's Christmas
Gifts for the New Year
Lincoln's library fine
Princess lonely heart
Washington's lucky star
White house rabbit
Baskets or bonnets
Merry-go-round for mother
Magic pencils

Miller, Helen L. First plays for children. Boston, Plays 1960.
Busy barbers
Broken broomstick
Spunky punky
Wishing stream
Library circus
Mother Goose bakeshop
Thankful's red beads
Thanksgiving riddle
Visit to Goldilocks
Lost Christmas cards
Wake up, Santa Claus
Real Princess
Safety clinic
Ten pennies for Lincoln
Country store cat
Wait & see
Shower of hearts
Weatherman on trial
Old Glory grows up
Garden hold-up
Rabbits who changed their minds
Trouble in Tick-tock town
May day for mother
Three little kittens
Teddy bear hero

Miller, Helen L. Gold medal plays for holidays, Boston, Plays, 1960
Greedy goblin
School for scaring
Mystery of Turkey-Lurkey
Strictly Puritan
Thanks to butter-finger
Mr. Snow-White's Christmas
Mary's invitation
Turning the tables
Miraculous tea party
Forgotten hero
Vicky gets the vote
Christmas umbrella
Softy the snowman

Bird's Christmas carol
Santa Claus twins
Christmas runaways
Santa Claus for president
Mystery at Knob Creek farm
Melody for Lincoln
Tree of hearts
Crosspatch & cupid
Washington shilling
Dolly saves the day
Washington's leading lady
Bunnies & bonnets
Bashful Bunny
Mother's fairy godmother
Magic carpet sweeper
Lacey's last garland
Talking flag

Miller, Helen, L. Modern plays for special days. Boston, Plays, 1965.

Curse of Hag Hollow
Haunts for hire
Damsels in distress
Horn of plenty
Broadway turkey
Red-carpet Christmas
Mistletoe mystery
Red flannel suit
Man like Lincoln
Valentine for Kate
Call Washington, 1776
General returns
Mother beats the band
Dial M for mother
Part-time hero
Gathering sticks

Miller, Sarah W. Acting out the truth. Nashville, Broadman, 1961.

We are witnesses
Go, ye faithful witnesses
Send the light
Unto one of these
Women to remember
Money talks
Come over to Macedonia
Let freedom ring
Blessed is the nation
He is risen
The cross
Birthday gift
The shepherds
Jonah

The sponsor
Thou art come to the kingdom
Love
I love you truly
God's available power
Create in me a clean heart, O God
Our God is creator
If a Bible talked
The point family
——— Modern skit & stunt book. Minneapolis, Denison, 1963.
Friday's Thursday off
How we started
Romeo & Juliet & their papas
What's in a name?
Kupid's College
Sheriff of Nottingham's nephew
Worrying around
Really significant poem
At the court of King April Fool
Mary Anne's mortgage
Hospital blues
Bus stop at Cactus Junction
If thoughts could speak
End it all
Don't put off being honest
Dog tricks
Nerve on display
Tragedy in rhyme
Memory course
Spirits on parade
Social climbing
Art is a wonderful thing
Big business
Wire trouble
One time table
Contest for two
Arrival in person
Through with girls
    Also many other short stunts and skits

Montano, Severino, ed. Prize winning plays of the Arena Theatre of the
    Philippines 1956-57. Quezon City, 1958.
Peralta, Jesus. Other son
Anchera, Augustina. Wife goes into politics
Flores, J. T. Flowers for the dead
    Also longer play.

Moon, Samuel. comp. One act. N. Y. Grove, 1961.
Strindberg. Miss Julie
Wilder, Thornton. Pullman Car Hiawatha
Yeats, W. B. Purgatory

Pirandello, Luigi. Man with the flower in his mouth
Saroyan, William. Hello out there
Williams, Tennessee. 27 wagons full of cotton
O'Casey, Sean. Bedtime story
Anouilh, Jean. Cecile
MacLeish, Archibald. This music crept by me upon the waters
Miller, Arthur. Memory of two Mondays
Ionesco, Eugene. The chairs

Murray, John. Comedies & farces for teen-agers. Boston, Plays, 1959.

Mish-mash bird
Rented tux
Valiant villain
I love you, Mr. Klotz
Lock, stock & barrel
Honest Injun
How hi is your fi?
Every room with bath
Colossal, stupendous
That's the spirit
Miss Hepplewhite takes over
Quiz biz
His & hers
Mr. Filbert's claim to fame
The perfect couple

Murray, John. Comedy roundup for teenage actors. Boston, Plays, 1964.

Badlands Ballyhoo
Mister twister
Take my advice
Invisible inventions, inc.
Belles of Horsefly gulch
Vote for Miss Checkout
Visitor from outer space
My host—the ghost
Shiver my timbers
Two for the money
Love's in fashion
Like mother used to make
Don't call us—we'll call you
Gray flannel blues
Kid avalanch

Murray, John. One-act plays for young actors. Minneapolis, Denison, 1959.

A letter to Sam
Home in the country
Mr. Mumbly's miracle
The well
One hundred dollars
Eenie, meenie, minee, murder!

Miss Hepplewhite & the general
Special services of Mr. Doodle
Italian love song
New Neighbor
Old lovers' ghosts
Miss Herkimer's missile

N

Neville, M. A. & Herzberg, M. J. Literature in America. Chicago, Rand, 1958.

Fletcher, Lucille. Sorry, wrong number
Sherwood, R. E. Abe Lincoln in Illinois
   Also other important material.

New Directions. Playbook. Norfolk, Conn, 1956.

Abel, Lionel. Death of Odysseus
Kinoshito, Junji. Twilight crane
Richards, I .A. Leak in the universe
   Also three longer plays.

Newman, Deborah. Holiday plays for little players. Boston, Plays, 1957.

Compass for Columbus
Fire-safe town
Something for Halloween
Pumpkin eaters' pumpkin
Election day, USA
Key to peace
Gift to the world
Emperor's new clothes
Aladdin
Real Princess
Thanks to the Indians
First Thanksgiving
Thanks for Thanksgiving
Best part of Christmas
Long ago in Bethlehem
Christmas tree surprise
Way to the inn
Christmas at the Cratchits
Happy holidays
Present for Abe
Mr. Lincoln's beard
Stolen heart
Somebody's valentine
Washington's gold button
New Washington
Prize shamrock
Magic goose
Bunny of the year
In honor of trees

Roses for mother
Stars & stripes
All-American tour

Nolan, P. T. Round the world for young people. Boston, Plays, 1961.
Double nine of Chih Yuan
Robin Hood & the match at Nottingham
French cabinet maker
Gates of Dinkelsbuehl
Skill of Pericles
Leak in the dike
Our sister, Sitya
Boshibari & the two thieves
Licha's birthday serenade
Golden voice of Little Erik
Stanislaw & the wolf
Highland fling
Magic of Salamanca
Son of William Tell
America is song
Johnny Appleseed
Christmas

O

O'Casey, Sean. Three plays. N. Y. St. Martins, 1961.
Figuro in the night
Moon shines on Kylenamore
    Also a longer play

Okun, Lillian. Let's listen to a story. N. Y. Wilson, 1959.
Field, Rachel. Polly Patchwork
Steele, W. O. Lone hunt
Barksdale, Lena. First Thanksgiving
Baker, Nina B. Young Abe Lincoln
Jackson, C. P. Two boys & a soap box derby
Kjelgaard, James. Danny meets Big Red
Pauli, Hertha. Silent night
Bishop, Claire. All alone
Carlson, Natalie S. Family under the bridge
Brooks, W. R. Freddy the detective
Neikirk, Mable E. Oscar on roller skates
Arabian Nights. Scheherazade tells the story of Sinbad

Olfson, Lewy. ed. Dramatized classics. Vol. I. Boston, Plays, 1964.
Dickens, Charles. Oliver Twist
Doyle, A. C. Sherlock Holmes & the Red-headed league
Sheridan, R. B. Rivals
Wells, H. G. Invisible man
Alcott, Louisa M. Little women
Hope, Anthony. Prisoner of Zenda

Moliere. Doctor in spite of himself
Homer. Odyssey
Chaucer. Canterbury tales
Carroll, Lewis. Alice in Wonderland
Hugo, Victor. Christmas for Cosette
Verne, Jules. 20,000 leagues under the sea

O'Neill, Eugene. Ten "lost" plays. N. Y. Random, 1964.
Thirst
The web
Warnings
Fog
Recklessness
Abortion
The movie man
The sniper
A wife for a life
    Also a longer play

Osborne, John. Plays for England. London, Faber, 1963.
Under plain cover
    Also longer play.

P

Pethybridge, D. C. Directed drama. London, Uni. of London, 1951.
Daughter of Pharaoh
Red cord
Spare a copper for the guy
    Also other material

Phillips, J. B. A man called Jesus. N. Y. Macmillan, 1959.
Gift of the holy spirit
The ascension
Jesus appears in Galilee
Jesus appears to his disciples
Resurrection of Jesus
Death of Jesus & the promise of resurrection
Trial before Pilate
Arrest in the garden
Last supper
Parable of the last judgment
Parable of the Pharisee & the tax collector
Boyhood of Jesus
Baptism of Jesus
Calling of the disciples
Temptation of Jesus
Cleansing of the temple
Christ enters Jerusalem
Journey to Jerusalem
Healing of the man born blind

Healing at the pool of Betheseda
Healing of the paralyzed man
The transfiguration
Christ the son of God
Centurion's servant
Jesus returns to Galilee
Lord's prayer

Plays Magazine. Vol. 22, Oct.—May, 1962-1963.

Many other volumes of plays. Only the above indexed in this bibliography.

Too many to be listed. Indexed in Reader's Guide to Periodical Literature, Address, 8 Arlington St. Boston, Mass.

Pooley, R. C. & others. Exploring life through literature. Chicago, Scott Foresman, 1957.

Tarkington, Booth. Trysting place
Hammerstein, Oscar II. Getting to know you
Jacob, W. W. Monkey's paw
Also much other material

Pooley, R. C. & others. Wide, wide world. Chicago, Scott Foresman, 1959.

Longstreth, Edward. Golden touch
Miller, Helen L. Soft-hearted ghost
Gilmore, Alice C. Lens maker
Also much material

Powers, V. E. ed. Nights of Noel. Evanston, Row Peterson, 1959.

Grandgeorge, William. The vision
Risser, A. C. A child for a King
Emblem, D. L. Nature of a gift
Phillips, Margaret K. Ever on Christmas Eve
Cooper, F. A. A certain star

Powers, V. E. ed. Plays for players. Evanston, Row Peterson, 1957.

Purkey, Ruth A. The leprechaun
Thompson, David. Shoemaker's wife
Smith, Betty. Lawyer Lincoln
Gould, J. R. Steps from beyond
Richter, Norma F. Hold onto your hat
Joy, R. P. Hour of honor
Wallace, Nancy. Speed bonnie boat
St. Clair, Robert. Miracle of the madonna
Olfson, Lewy. Infanta
Estrada, Doris. Three on a bench
Love, C. R. Proof of a man
Vining, Donald. One that got away
Coyle, R. W. Unto thy doors
Powers, Verne. The wall
Kuekel, W. A. Sunstroke
Robinson, C. R. White dove

Greene, N. D. Seekers
  Also valuable material on play production.

Pratt, Lois H. The Puppet do-it-yourself book. N. Y. Exposition, 1957.
  Goldilocks & the three bears
  Little bear tries to see Santa Claus
  Pirate's treasure chest

Q

Quinlan, M. Eva. Plays for early teens. N. Y. Baker, 1958.
  Dorothea dances the minuet
  Final rehearsal
  Boston tea party
  Pan of candy
  Why mothers get gray
  Hiding places

R

Rees, Lester. ed. Mask & microphone. Sydney, Australia, Bridge, 1963.
  Euripides. Alcestis
  Hsiung, S. I. Lady Precious Stream

Reeves, James. Peddler's dream & other plays. N. Y. Dutton, 1963.
  Peddler's dream
  Mulcaster market
  Stolen boy

Reinnert, Otto. ed. Drama. Boston, Little, 1961.
  Strindberg, August. Ghost sonata
  Yeats, W. B. Purgatory
  Brecht, Bertolt. Good woman of Setzuan
  Ionesco, Eugene. The lesson
    Also longer play.
  Barrie, J. M. The will
  Palmer, Vance. Blackhorse
  Corwin, Norman. Plot to overthrow Christmas
  MacLeish, Archibald. Fall of the city
    Also other material.

Reines, Bernard J. For country & mankind. N. Y. Longmans, 1944.
  The making of Mark Twain
  Citizen Franklin of Philadelphia
  So precious a gift
  Pulitzer of the "World"
  Audubon makes his decision
  Walter Scott's American guest
  Clara Barton, Lady of Mercy
  Edison's light
  From this small beginning

Horace Mann, American educator
Louis Pasteur
Rizal of the Philippines

Richardson, Willis. King's dilemma & other plays for children. N. Y. Exposition, 1956.
King's dilemma
Dragon's tooth
Gypsy's finger ring
Near calvary
New Santa Claus
Man of magic

S

St. Clair. Robert. Religious plays for amateur players. Minneapolis, Denison, 1964.
As we forgive
Light within
And lose his own soul
Fresh start for the Beales
Probable sons
The William Tyndale story
The story of Jedediah Smith
Taming of the shrew
Stolen blessing
Whither thou goest
Who shall be the Madonna?
Christmas candle
Children's Christmas pageant
Pilgrim Thanksgiving service
Legend beautiful
Orphan's mite

Sando, Esther G. A pair of gloves. Philadelphia. Christian Education, 1962.
Pair of gloves
Granny's rose
Our spiritual food
Handmaid of God
Holy experiment
Wondrous gift
Asher, the camel boy
Prince Boniface discovers Christmas
O come to my heart
Loving-giving
Come down
The wall

Sartoris, Ramon. Three plays. Washington, Black Sun, 1944.
If Caesar be

Clue of the wrong thing
From core to rind

Schneideman, Rose. Radio plays for young people to act. N. Y. Dutton, 1961.
No-tax island
Change of mind
Best citizens of our town
Hands across the sea
Soldiers of peace
Love your neighbors
Santa strikes back
This is New York
Program for peace
Melting pot
Crossroads to education

Schramm, Wilbur & others. Adventure for Americans. N. Y. Harcourt, 1956.
O'Neill, Eugene. Ile
Zone of quiet
   Also long play & other material

Segal, Samuel M. On stage everyone. N. Y. Jonathan David, 1957.
Voices of the Shofarim
It happened on Kol Nidre night
Kite fell in the Sukkah
Chanukah lights & satellites
Chanukah on a mystery planet
Super light Hanukah
Purim puppets
Achash veros, incorporated
Lady Esther from Shushaiyen
Purim dragnet
Vashtirams
Syncopated Seder
Great Charoses
Silent watchmen
Walls have ears
Clock that rested
Shooting Chanukah
S S Tikvah

Serling, Rod. Patterns. N. Y. Simon & Schuster, 1957.
Patterns
Requiem for a heavyweight
The rack
Old MacDonald had a curve
   Also commentaries on writing for television

Settel, Irving, comp. Best television humor of the year. N. Y. Wyn, 1956.
Benny, Jack. Jack Benny's program

Bendix, William. Life of Riley
Moore, Garry. Garry Moore show
Berg, Gertrude. Goldbergs
Nelson, Harriet & Ozzie. Adventures of Ozzie & Harriet
Como, Perry. Perry Como show
Raye, Martha. Martha Raye show
Cummings, Bob. Bob Cummings show
Paar, Jack. Jack Paar show
Colman, Ronald. Halls of Ivy
   Also three monologues.

Shaw, G. B. Seven one-act plays. Baltimore, Penguin, 1958.
Man of destiny
How he lied to her husband
Passion, Poison, petrifaction
Dark lady of the sonnets
Overruled
Admiral Bashville
Village wooing

Shaw, G. B. The shorter plays. N. Y. Dodd, 1960.
Why she would not
Shakes versus Shav
Six of Calais
Annajouska, the Bolshevik Empress
Augustus does his bit
Inca of Jerusalem
O'Flaherty, V. C.
Shewing-up of Blanco Poset

Sister M. Genevieve. Plays for grade & High school children.
   N. Y. Exposition, 1956.
A court, a Queen & the Church
Christmas in the mountain chapel
Seasons come & go

Sloane, Gertrude G. Fun with folktales. N. Y. Dutton, 1942.
King Thrushbeard
Golden goose
Rumpelstiltskin
Sprig of rosemary
Little red hen & the grain of wheat
Who laughs last laughs best

Smith, Moyne R. Plays & how to put them on. N. Y. Walck, 1961.
Arthur's sword
Suppose
Potted Princess
Magic fishbone
Reluctant dragon
Great Quillow
Necklace of Princess Fiorimonde

Smith, R. G. Boy's entertainment book. Minneapolis, Denison, 1957.

Be prepared
Slight misunderstanding
Comrad Justice
Ham actor
Going home from the dance
Just made it
Heavy Chiffonier
Hot cakes
Where's grandpa
Love that tractor
Dumb sentry
Greek merchant & the lions
Handy man
Too much Mary Jane
Why, Daddy?
No deal
Smith brothers cough drops
Sweet revenge
Susie
Susie wonders
Tall, dark & Handsome
Burning schoolhouse
Aloysius Bigmouth
School days
    Also stunts & other entertainment

Somerscales, Marjorie. Fourteen short plays for young players. London, Pitman, 1962.

Minstrels
Border raid
Twelve days of Christmas
Get up & bar the door
In dulci Jubilo
Death of giant despair
Forty winks
Lost birds
Toy's revolt
The Corsair
Young Lochinvar
1804 (Napoleonic Wars)
Runaway chimney sweep

Spark, Muriel. Voices at play. Philadelphia, Lippincott, 1962.

Danger zone
Dry river bed
The interview
The party through the wall
    Also six short stories.

Strindberg, August. Five plays of Strindberg. N. Y. Doubleday. 1960.

Creditors

Great highways
  Also three longer plays.

T

Tichenor, Tom. Folk plays for puppets you can make. Nashville, Abingdon, 1959.
  The three Billy Goats Gruff
  The Princess who could not cry
  The city mouse & the country mouse
  Simpleton
  The little red hen

Turgenev, Ivan. Three famous plays. N. Y. Hill & Wang, 1959.
  A provincial lady
    Also two longer plays.

U

Ulanov, Barry. Makers of the modern drama. N. Y. McGraw-Hill, 1961.
  Miller, Arthur. View from the bridge
  O'Neill, Eugene. Long voyage home
  Ionesco, Eugene. Bald soprano
  Yeats, W. B. Purgatory
  Yeats, W. B. On Baile's strand
    Also many long plays, & material about the drama.

V

Very, Alice. Round the clock plays for children. Boston, Plays, 1957.
  Three little kittens go to school
  Puss-in-boots
  Return of Columbus
  Little friends
  Cat who wanted to ride on a broom
  Old Lady Witch's party
  Dancing children
  Cock & the fox
  Thanksgiving eve
  Jonathan's Thanksgiving
  Too much turkey
  Getting ready for winter
  The snow girl
  Dr. Time's office
  Shoemaker & the elves
  Everywhere Christmas
  Little fir tree
  The twelve months
  Jack & the beanstalk
  Abe Lincoln goes to school
  Valentine sale

St. Valentine's surprise
The callers
General George
King Winter
Fairy circus
The old woman & her pig
Three sillies
Trees at school
The Mayflower
Golden bell for mother
John Grumlie
Flower garden
Planting time

W

Wallerstein, J. S. Adventure, five plays for youth. N. Y. Bellamy, 1956.
Windigo island
Bobby & the time machine
Cactus wildcat
Johnny Aladdin
  Also one longer play.

Ward, R. H. ed. Ten peace plays. London, Dent. n.d.
Russell, Eileen. All quiet in the air
Flather, Horace. Jonathan's day
Armstrong, J. Eleventh hour
Arlett, Vera I. Door was closed
Victor, Robert. Pen is mightier
Grant, Neil. Last war
Pollock, J. On the frontier
Box, Sydney. Not this man
Barling, Edith M. The Governor
Steinmetz, Martha. Tarakin

Weiss, S. A. ed. Drama in the modern world. Boston, Heath, 1964.
Strindberg, August. Miss Julie
Williams, Tennessee. Glass menagerie
Ionesco, Eugene. Bald soprano
Beckett, Samuel. All that fall
Arbuzov, Alexei. It happened in Irkutsk
  Also many longer plays, and drama information.

Williams, Charles. Collected plays. London, Oxford, 1963.
Thomas Cranmer of Canterbury
Seed of Adam
Death of Good Fortune
House by the stable
Grab & grace
Terror of light

Three temptations
  Also longer plays.

Z

Zachar, J. J. ed. Plays as experience. Rev. N. Y. Odyssey, 1963.
  McCarty, Sara S. Three's a crowd
  Niggli, Josephina. Ring of General Macias
  Chekhov, Anton. The boor
  Field, Rachel. 15th candle
  Finch, Robert. Goodbye to Lazy K
  Benet, S. V. Devil & Daniel Webster
  Truex, James. Sounds of triumph
  Kozlenko, William. Jacob comes home
  Hall, Holworthy. Valiant
  Conkle, E. P. Sparkin'
  Goodman, K. S. Back of the yards
  Wilde, Percival. Pawns
  Glaspell, Susan. Trifles

SUBJECT LIST

ACCIDENTS

Fright

ACTING

Audition is over
Final rehearsal
First rehearsal
Glamour
Ham actor
Ham that am (The)
Nobody knows
Reversal in rehearsal
Sound effects man
Their first play

ACTORS

Flattering word

ACTRESS

Curtains
First scene

ADAPTATIONS

Alcott—Happy holidays for Little women
Alcott—Little women
Andersen—Emperor's new clothes
Andersen—Emperor's nightingale
Andersen—Real Princess
Arabian Nights—Aladdin
Arabian Nights—Ali Baba & the 40 thieves
Arabian Nights—Scheherazade kept on talking
Arabian Nights—Scheherazade tells the story of
    Sinbad
Atwater—Mr. Popper's penguins
Baum—Wizard of Oz
Bible, Old Testament—Cain & Abel
Bible, Old Testament—Prologue to King David
Bunyan—Trial of the faithful
Burnett—Little Princess
Burnett—Racketty-packetty house
Carroll—Alice in wonderland

185

Carroll—Mad tea party
Carroll—Through the looking glass
Cervantes—Don Quixote saves the day
Chaucer—Canterbury tales
Dickens—Magic fishbone
Dickens—Oliver Twist
Dickens—Oliver Twist asks for more
Doyle—Sherlock Holmes & the red-headed league
Dumas—Treasure of Monte Cristo
Field—Coming of the Prince
Grahame—Reluctant dragon
Greek myths—Apple of discord
Strange tale of King Midas
Grimm—Gift to the world
Grimm—Golden goose
Grimm—Shoemaker & the elves
Hardy—Second stranger
Hardy—Tony Kytes, the arch deceiver
Hawthorne—Dr. Heidegger's experiment
Homer—Odyssey
Hope—Prisoner of Zenda
Howells—Christmas every day
Hugo—Bishop's candlesticks
Hugo—Christmas for Cosette
Irving—Return of Rip van Winkle
King Arthur—Galahad & the maidens
Kipling—Potted Princess
Lang—Sprig of rosemary
Mark Twain—Adventure of Tom Sawyer
Mark Twain—Tom Sawyer's morning
Moliere—Doctor in spite of himself
Poe—Three Sundays in a week
Pyle—Staff & the fiddle
Sachs—Shoemaker's wife
Scott—Young Lochinvar
Shakespeare—Romeo & Juliet
Sheridan—Rivals
Swift—Gulliver wins his freedom
Thurber—Great Quillow
Tolstoi—What men live by
Verne—Around the world—by way of America
Verne—20,000 leagues under the sea
Wells—Invisible man
Wilde—Infanta
Wyss—Swiss family Robinson—rescued

ADVENTURE

Robin Hood in Sherwood forest
Johnny Appleseed in danger

ADOLESCENTS

Portrait of Nelson Holiday, Jr.

ADVERTISING

Gray flannel blues
Madison Ave. merry-go-round

AFFAIRS

Her affairs in order

AIRPLANE

All American tour
Back seat pilot
Girdle round the earth

ALCHEMIST

Jest of Hahalaba

ALCOHOLISM

Distant thunder

ALLEGORY

Seekers

ANIMALS

Home sweet home
From this small beginning

ANTIQUES

George Washington's chair
Purple door knob
Word of honor

APARTMENT LIFE

Castle in the Village

APRIL FOOL DAY

At the court of King April Fool
Magic goose

ARBOR DAY

Forest fantasy
In honor of trees
Trees at school

ARMY

Rack (The)

ARRIVAL

Arrival in person

ART

Art alliance
Art is a wonderful thing
Thing of beauty

ARTIST

Bill, the matchmaker

ASTRONOMY

Be prepared

ATHLETICS, COLLEGE

Strains of triumph
Will to win

ATOMIC RESEARCH

Miss Herkimer's missile

AUCTION

Country auction

AUTOGRAPH

Autograph, please
To Bobolink, for her spirit

AUTOMOBILE

Used car for sale
Bab buys a car
Bent fender
It's her or the car

BABY

Bauble for the baby
Where's the baby?

BABY SITTER

Baby sitter
Baby sitters
Negotiations
Sitting tonight

BACKWOODS

Bride comes to Yellow Sky

BAKE CONTEST

Like mother used to make

BALL

After the ball

BALLOON

Runaway balloon

BANK

Is thrift a virtue?

BARBER

Bargains in haircuts
Brown man's burden
Busy barbers
Gay nineties barber shop

BASEBALL

Daylight saving
It's a silly game
Johnny on the spot
Kill the ump
Old Mac Donald had a curve
Stay awake

BE KIND TO ANIMALS WEEK

Love your neighbor

BEATNIKS

Beatnik & the bard
Nude washing dishes

BEGGAR

Spare a copper for the guy

BEAUTY

Beauty is fled
Beauty parade
Beauty shop
Thing of beauty
Venus beauty factory

BIOGRAPHY

Jane Addams—Jane Addams
Aesop—Aesop, man of fables
Appleseed—Apples in the wilderness
Appleseed—Johnny Appleseed
Appleseed—Johnny Appleseed's vision
Appleseed—Sound of apples
Benedict Arnold—Not for sale
John Jacob Astor—Astor's bid for empire
Audubon—Audubon makes his decision
Clara Barton—Angel of the battlefield
Clara Barton—Clara Barton
Clara Barton—Clara Barton, lady of mercy
Clara Barton—For soldiers everywhere
Anne Boleyn—Mistress Minx
Edwin Booth—Final performance
Nathaniel Bowditch—Nathaniel Bowditch, the
    navigator
Governor Bradford—Thanks to the Indians
Jim Bridger—Jim Bridger & his eight-hour echo
Buddha—Tsunemasa
Caesar—J Caesar
Columbus—Admiral
Columbus—Admiral's nightmare
Columbus—Landing of Columbus
Columbus—Most memorable voyage
Columbus—Near mutiny on the Santa Maria
Columbus—Sailing west to find the east
Columbus—This music crept by me upon the waters
Thomas Cranmer—Thos. Cranmer of Canterbury
Davy Crockett—With sunrise in his pocket
Edison—Edison's light
Eugene Field—Gay poet
Franklin—B. Franklin

Franklin—Ben Franklin, peacemaker
Franklin—Benjamin Franklin
Franklin—Citizen Franklin of Philadelphia
Franklin—Out in the rain again
Gauguin—Noa, noa
Hillel—Hillel the student
Hitler—Jacob comes home
Hitler—Return to Berchtesgaden
Sam Houston—Sam Houston
Washington Irving—Walter Scott's American guest
Jeanne D'Arc— Jeanne D'Arc
Jefferson—Ask Mr. Jefferson
Jefferson—Out to win
Jefferson—Thomas Jefferson
Jonah—It should happen to a dog
Robert E. Lee—Robert E. Lee
Lincoln—Gift of Laughter
Lincoln—Honest Abe Lincoln
Lincoln—Lincoln reckons up
Lincoln—Lincoln's library fine
Lincoln—Lonesome train
Lincoln—Mole on Lincoln's cheek
Lincoln—Picture in the fire
Lincoln—With malice toward none
Lincoln—Young Abe Lincoln
Mary Todd Lincoln—One love had Mary
Charles A. Lindbergh—Soloist
Dolly Madison—Daring, darling Dolly
Horace Mann—Horace Mann, American educator
Mark Twain—Making of Mark Twain
Margaret of Scotland—A court, a Queen & the
   Church
Moses Mendelsohn—Unlighted Menorah
Anna Cora Mowatt—Leading lady
Napoleon—Man of destiny
Napoleon—Nerve of Napoleon
Florence Nightingale—As moths unto the lamp
Annie Oakley—Straight shooter
Pasteur—Louis Pasteur
William Penn—William Penn
Peter the Great—Lens maker
Pocahontas—Historical hystericals
Pocahontas—Pocahontas
Pulitzer—Pulitzer of "The World"
Walter Reed—Yellow fever
Paul Revere—Paul Revere
Betsy Ross— Brave new banner
Betsy Ross—Washington's lucky star
Sacajawea—Sacajawea
Mother Seton—Seasons come and go
Shakespeare—Dark lady of the sonnets

Shakespeare—Landslide for Shakespeare
Captain John Smith—True story of Cap't. John
   Smith
Socrates—Prologue to an unfinished play
Miles Standish—Bartholomew's joyous noise
Harriet Beecher Stowe—Prelude to fame
Peter Stuyvesant—23 & Regina
Swift—Dreaming dust
Titus—Bar Giora
William Tyndal—William Tyndal story
Van Gogh—Era of Vincent van Gogh
Jules Verne—One way for another
Queen Victoria—Bell (The)
Queen Victoria—Domestic differences
Queen Victoria—Extremes meet
Queen Victoria—Heavy change
Queen Victoria—Life in the Highlands
Queen Victoria—Order of preference
Queen Victoria—Popular voice
Queen Victoria—Recollections
Queen Victoria—Ruling powers
Queen Victoria—Superlative relative
Queen Victoria—This is the heir
Queen Victoria—Visit to Birmingham
Leonardo da Vinci—Man who lived too soon
Washington—George Washington
Daniel Webster—Daniel Webster
John Wesley—John Wesley
Marcus Whitman—Answering the call
Wright brothers—Kitty Hawk—1903

BIRDS

Bird in the bush
Lost birds
Mish-mosh birds
Starling

BLACK SHEEP

Ant & the grasshopper

BLANK VERSE

Admirable Bashville

BOARDING HOUSE

Don't call us—we'll call you
McMumbly's miracle

BOOK WEEK

Aladdin steps out
Alice in Bookland
Book magic
Books are bridges
Bunch of keys
Case for books
Damsels in distress
Library circus
Man behind the book
Miraculous tea party
Parrot & the pirates
Runaway unicorn
Turning the tables

BOOKS

Fortune of Merrylegs & Tawny-whiskers
Use the book

BOOR

The Boor

BOY MEETS GIRL

Afterwards

BRIDGE

Five brothers

BROADCAST

Mister Twister

BUBBLE GUM

Help wanted—badly

BURGLAR

Good night, Caroline

BUS

Bus stops at Cactus junction
Heat lightning
People in the wind
Playful bus

On vengeance heights
Sammy
She walks in beauty
Shirkers
Sisters McIntosh
Speed bonnie boat
Still stands the old house
This way to heaven
Three to get married
27 wagons full of cotton
What men live by

CHARITY BAZAAR

Mrs. Harper's bazaar

CHARM SCHOOL

Charm racket

CHILDREN

Rainy afternoon
Three people

CHOICE

Why she would not

CHRISTMAS

Adobe Christmas
All aboard for Christmas
And Christmas is its name
Best part of Christmas
Boy with a cart
Bundles for Christmas
Calling all Christmases
Chosen one
Christmas apples
Christmas at check point Charlie
Christmas at mother's
Christmas at the Cratchits
Christmas at the Gables
Christmas awakening
Christmas barricade
Christmas bug
Christmas coast to coast
Christmas cowboy
Christmas in court
Christmas in Quarantine
Christmas in the market place

Say it with rhymes
Scrooge
Search for the Savior
Shoes & stockings for Solomon
Softy the snow man
Something in the air
Squeaknibble's Christmas
Three skits for Christmas
Tidings of joy
To us a son
Touchstone
Twelve days of Christmas
Twinkle
Video Christmas
Vision
Way (The)
Week before Christmas
What's for Christmas
White Christmas
Why the chimes rang

CHRISTMAS CANDLES

Candles for Christmas
Christmas candles

CHRISTMAS EVE

Christmas eve dream
Christmas eve letter
Ever on Christmas eve
Knight before Christmas
'Twas the night before Christmas

CHRISTMAS FLOWERS

Christmas rose
Legend of the Christmas rose
Violets for Christmas

CHRISTMAS GIFTS

Birthday gift
Christmas gift
Gift for old Saint Nick
Greatest gift
Just a little something for Christmas
Loving-giving
Mrs. Claus' Christmas present
Nature of a gift
Saint (The)
Wondrous gift

CHRISTMAS GREETINGS

Merry Christmas, Crawfords
Merry Christmas customs
Merry Christmas elf
Merry Christmas in the old home town
Season's greetings

CHRISTMAS MIRACLE

Christmas miracle
Miracle for Mary
Miracle of the Madonna

CHRISTMAS NATIVITY

Birthplace for a King
Guardian
Inn of Bethlehem
Long ago in Bethlehem
No room at the inn
O little town of Bethlehem
On such a night
Road to Bethlehem
Room for a King
Room for Mary
Seed of Adam
Stable at midnight
Unto thy doors
Who shall be the Madonna?

CHRISTMAS PAGEANT

Children's Christmas pageant
Old fashioned English Christmas

CHRISTMAS—SANTA CLAUS

Holiday for Santa
Left-over reindeer
Monsieur Santa Claus
New Santa Claus
Reindeer on the roof
Santa & the spaceman
Santa Claus
Santa Claus for President
Santa Claus twins
Santa strikes back
Second marriage of Santa Claus
Setting Santa straight
Standing up for Santa
Uncle Santa Claus

Wake up Santa Claus
What, no Santa Claus?

CHRISTMAS SHEPHERDS

Littlest shepherd
Shepherd who stayed
Shepherds
Way to the inn

CHRISTMAS SONGS

And a song was born
Bell of St. Hildegarde
Bird's Christmas carol
Christmas carol
Gift of music
Silent night
Sing the songs of Christmas
Song in the night
Star song

CHRISTMAS SPIRIT

Christmas spirit
Spirit of Christmas
Where's your Christmas spirit?

CHRISTMAS STAR

Certain star
Christmas star for Olga

CHRISTMAS TOYS

Runaway toys
Toy shop
What happened in Toyland

CHRISTMAS TREE

Christmas tree surprise
Enchanted Christmas tree
First Christmas tree
Little Chip's Christmas tree
Little fir tree
Talking Christmas tree
This way to Christmas
Tiniest Christmas tree
Tree to trim
Trimming the tree
Up a Christmas tree

COLUMBUS DAY

Admiral's nightmare
Boy dreamer
Compass for Columbus
Glory he deserves
Return of Columbus
Return of the Nina
To the new world

COMMITTEE MEETING

Entertainment committee

COMMUNISM

Comrad justice

CONEY ISLAND

Mermaid avenue is the world

CONTEST

Contest by two

CONVICTS

Hymn to the rising sun
Moon up

COSMETICS

Miss Hepplewhite takes over

COUNTRIES

Africa—Arrest (The)
Africa—Dry river bed
Africa—We commit this body
Africa—With General Wow in darkest Africa
Alaska—Sourdough Sally
Australia—Black horse
Canada—Neighbors to the North
Canada—Two sides of darkness
Chile—Express for Santiago
Cyprus—Airmail from Cyprus
China—Battle of wits
China—Double 9 of Chih Yuan
China—Good woman of Setzuan
China—Lady Precious Stream
China—Lost Princess

China—Mrs. Charlie Chan
China—Pear tree
China—Romance of the willow pattern
China—Stolen Prince
Druids—Druid's ring
East Berlin—Fear is a murderer
Egypt (ancient)—Sokar & the crocodile
France—French cabinet maker
France—Humulus, the mute
France—Farce of the worthy Master Pierre Patelin
France—Mirror-wardrobe one fine evening
Germany—Gates of Dinkelsbuehl
Germany—Merry Tyll
Germany—Wandering scholar from paradise
Greece (ancient)—First Mrs. Paris
Hawaii—Aloha, mother
Holland—Leak in the dike
Holland—Small shoes & small tulips
Indonesia—Our sister, Sitya
Ireland—Cathleen ni Houlihan
Ireland—Figuro in the night
Ireland—Leprechaun
Ireland—Mad islands
Ireland—Miracle of the boar
Ireland—On Baile's strand
Ireland—Purgatory
Ireland—Riders to the sea
Ireland—Rising of the moon
Ireland—Spreading the news
Israel—Eliezer Ben Yehudah
Israel—Herzel comes home
Israel—It happened on Kol Nidre night
Israel—Jerusalem
Israel—My cousin Avigdor
Israel—To the young—a vision
Italy—Bilora
Italy—Courters
Italy—Florentine tragedy
Japan—Abstraction
Japan—Atsumori
Japan—Boshibari
Japan—Dwarf trees
Japan—Heavenly robe of feathers
Japan—Kagekiyo
Japan—Nakamitsu
Japan—Protest
Japan—Twilight crane
Mexico—Dulce man
Mexico—Licha's birthday serenade
Mexico—Sunday costs five pesos
Mexico—This bull ate nutmeg

Mexico—Tooth or shave
Norway—Golden voice of little Erik
Nova Scotia—Phantom ship
Pan America—Honoring friendship
Philippines—Among the faithless
Philippines—Angry sea
Philippines—Cadaver
Philippines—Cristina goes with goats
Philippines—Dancers
Philippines—Finishing touches
Philippines—Goodby, my gentle
Philippines—Return of the warrior
Philippines—Roots
Philippines—Sa pula, sa puti
Philippines—Sabina
Philippines—Scent of fear
Philippines—Shadow & Solitude
Philippines—Summer funeral
Philippines—Technique is the thing
Philippines—Three of them
Philippines—Three rats
Philippines—Wife goes into politics
Philippines—World is an apple
Poland—Stanislaw & the wolf
Rome (ancient)—Captives
Rome—Greek merchant & the lions
Rome—Phormio
Rome—Traitor's reward
Russia—Game of chess
Russia—It happened in Irkutsk
Russia—Marriage proposal
Russia—Provincial lady
Scotland—Highland fling
Siam—Getting to know you
Spain—Cave of Salamanca
Spain—Magic of Salamanca
Spain—Sunny morning
Sweden—Creditors
Switzerland—Son of William Tell
West Indies—Emperor Jones

COUNTRY STORE

Country store cat
White tablecloth

COURT

Man versus dog
Order in the court
Rufus Robin's day in court

COWBOYS

Blue hotel
Get along little cowboy
Half pint cowboy
Jiminy Cinders
Sing the songs of cowboys
Tall Bill & his big ideas

CRIME

Giant stair
Web (The)

CRUISE

Winter cruise

CRYING

Don't cry, baby

DANCE

Boat Club dance
Charleston craze
Dancing school
Dorothea dances the minuet
Touch of fancy

DATING (TEEN)

Boy upstairs
Buddy buys an orchid
Date with Patsy

DEAF & DUMB

So you won't talk?

DEATH

Alcestis
Architruc
Best way to die
Dear departed
End of the story
Family album
Gone tomorrow
Journal of Vera Grey
Passion, poison, petrifaction

Room for death
Sandbox
Till death do us part

DEBTS

We Brents pay our debts

DECISION

Decision (The)

DEPARTMENT STORE

Keep smiling
Perfect couple

DETECTIVE

Affair in the park
Crime Club
Defective detective
Freddy the detective
Long shot
One of us

DEVIL

Change for the worst
Devil & Daniel Webster

DIETING

Counting the calories
Diet begins tomorrow

DINNER

Five in judgment
Patterson dinner

DIVORCE

Amicable parting
Divorce granted
Shadow play

DOCTOR

Emergency doctor
Herbert's hurt
Hurry, doctor
Mills that grind

DOG

Danny meets Big Red
Dog tracks
Double talk
Ginger Pye

DOLLARS

One hundred dollars

DOMESTIC

At the turn of the road
Farewell to Calvin
Greetings from the Fultons
Instructions for Gary
Johnny Nightmare
Keep it under cover
Luncheon for three
Miss Fix-it
No treat for Gilbert
Take care, Anne
Two for the show

DOOR

By your hand

DOPE

Dope

DOVE

White dove

DOZEN

Baker's dozen

DRAGON

Mail order dragon

DREAMS

Administrator
Dearie, you're a dreamer
Midsummer Night's play
Peddler's dream

DRESS

Pink & patches

DRUG STORE

At the corner drug store

DULLNESS

Life is so dull

EDUCATION

Change of mind
Daughter of the gods
Educating Josefina
Facing the future
Halls of Ivy
Honored one
Know the truth
Magic pencils
Mary's invitation
Resignation

EGO

Male model

ELECTION DAY

Vicky gets the votes
Vote for your hero

ELEVATOR

Little prison

ELOPEMENT

Let's get out of here

EMOTIONS

Heaven is a long time to wait

ENTERTAINMENT

Cleopatra, the second
Crimson feather
Curtain capers

Don't get excited
Duchess of Dogwood Lane
Have a good time
In the land of Schmozz
Just who is crazy?
Miss Hepplewhite & the general
No tears for Henry
Oscar on roller skates
Ready for Robert
Real Princess
Snow White
Wait & see
Who knocks?

ETHICAL

Hour of truth
Wages of sin

EYES

An eye-opener

FABLE

Cock & the fox

FAIR

Robin Hood & the match at Nottingham

FAIRY

Adalimina's pearl
Emperor's nightingale
Glass slipper
Hansel & Gretel
Jack & the beanstalk
Land of heart's desire
Little Red Riding Hood
Magic goose
Miss Muffet's wish
Plum blossom & the dragon
Princess is sorry
Princess lonely heart
Princess too little
Reluctant dragon
Rumpelstiltskin
Visit to Goldilocks

FAITH

Faith hawker

FALSE ACCUSATION

Souls in torment

FAMILY LIFE

Big hunt
Departing (The)
Do I bother you?
Eldest (The)
Expanding trade
Family tree
Five dollar bill
Fumed oak
Hand-me-down
Happy journey to Trenton
Haunted clothesline
Her majesty comes home
Last of the Lowries
Mother remembers
Orphans
Pan of candy
Sun is a dead man's weapon
To the lovely Margaret
Turn of the century
When altars burn
Who laughs last laughs best
Why mothers get grey

FANTASY

Dragon who giggled
Feathertop
Frosty, the snow man
Happy pagan
Heidi
Peter Cottontail
Steadfast tin soldier
Trial of Silver Fox
Worlds apart

FARMERS

Bread
Competition
Efficient expert
Fixins
Golden axe

FISH

One that got away
Tridget of Greva

FLAG DAY

Stars & stripes
Talking flag

FLATTERY

Flattering word

FLOWERS

Flower garden
Flowers & weeds
Flowers for the dead
Queen's flowers
Red carnations

FOG

Fog

FOLKPLAY

Devil & Daniel Webster
How boots befooled the King
John Grumlie
Kettle of brains
King Thrushbeard

FOOTBALL

End of the line
Kick off (The)
Some interference!
What a game! What a game!
What a mess

FORESTER

Ranger takes a wife

FORTUNE TELLER

Tall, dark & handsome

FOUNTAIN OF YOUTH

Fountains of youth

Stolen submarine
Thief in the house
Tragedy of the sea
When the West was young
Where is my wandering boy tonight!

GENERAL STORE

Mind over matter

GEOGRAPHY

This changing world

GHOST

Camp ghost
Dark walkers
Dilly dehaunting agency
Ghosts a la mode
Ghost by request
Ghost of Caesar's hair
Ghost of laughing Dan
Ghosts on strike
Good ghosts
Happy ending of a gruesome ghost
Headless horseman
Highland lad
Hitch-hiker
Indignant ghost
Madame Dode
My host—the ghost
Return of Michael Conley
Three squeals for freedom
Two ghosts are better than one
Vacant room
Your rooms are ready

GIFTS

Anybody's gift
Mr. Flannery's ocean

GIGOLO

Gigolo & gigolette

GIRL SCOUT

B girls extra
Beacon of strength

Heroine of Wren
"Molly Pitcher"
Needle fights for freedom
On the road to Yorktown
Our great Declaration
U.S.A. Frontier—Elisha & the Long Knives
Golden touch
Hold back the Redskins
John Jewitt, the slave
Statehood for Washington
Take-off
Territory is born
Through Natchez Pass
Toehold for the USA
Too many cooks
U.S.A. Civil War—Clod
U.S.A., Spanish War—Rizal of the Philippines
U.S.A. World War I—Sniper
U.S.A. World War II—Command decision
Four Chaplains
Red herrings
U.S.A. War Bond Drive—Awakening of Johnny
Castle
Ballet of Bataan
Bishop of Munster
Chicago, Germany
Christmas letter to the German people
Education for death
Education for life
Education for victory
Face of America
I saw the lights go out in Europe
I speak for the women of America
Jarvis Bay
Lesson in Japanese
Letter from a Red Army man
Miss Liberty goes to town
Modern Scrooge
Mrs. Murgatroyd's dime
Nightmare at noon
Paris incident
Price of Free World victory
Report on the state of the nation
Silent women
Snow goose
So long, son
Statue of Liberty
Wanted; a ballad
U.S.A. Citizenship—John Crown's legacy
We, the people
U.S.A. Election—Election day in the USA

HOLLYWOOD

HOME DECORATION

HOME LIFE

HONESTY

Don't put off being honest

HORSE & BUGGY DAYS

Days gone by
Livery stable

HOSPITAL

His sister
Hospital blues
Ladies-in-waiting
Operations
Safety clinic
You look ghastly
Zone of quiet

HOTEL

Day of departure
Every room with bath
Letter to Sam
Oh! waitress
Runaway

HUMAN GREED

27 wagons full of cotton

HUNGER

Where's grandpa?

HUNTERS

Hunted (The)
Lone hunt

HUSBAND & WIFE

George
Henry, the model husband
High pressure

IDEAS

Overpraised season

IMAGINATION

Frog Prince
Greta & the Prince
Necklace of Princess Florimonde

IMPERSONATION

Ugly duckling

IMPOSTERS

Divine spark

INCOME TAX

No-tax island

INDIAN LIFE & TALES

Cold face and warm heart
Dancing children
Honest Injun!
Gift of corn
Medicine man
No deals
Star that never moves
When the fire dies

INSANE ASYLUM

Gloria mundi

INSECTS

Storm is breaking

INTRIGUE

Still life

INVENTIONS

Apollo of Bellac
Bobby & the time machine
Daughters of invention
Invisible inventions, inc.

INVITATION

Social event

ISLANDS

Friday's Thursday off
Terror on the island

JEALOUSY

Wholesale jealousy

JEWS—HOLIDAYS

Chanukah—Chanukah lights & satellites
        Chanukah on a mystery planet
        Little candle that wouldn't
        Night before Chanukah
        Shooting Chanukah
        Super light Chanukah
Kol Nidre
        It happened on Kol Nidre night
Passover
        Passover story
        Syncopated Seder
Purim
        Purim dragnet
        Purim puppets
        Song for Queen Esther
        Vashtirama
        Vote for Haman!
Rosh Hashana
        Holiday minstrels
Shavuot
        Shavuot day dreams
Sukkot
        Going to a party
        Kite fell in the Sukkah
Jews—life & culture
        Achosh Veros, inc.
        Bespoke overcoat
        Brother Sam
        Clock that rested
         Comrades all
        Freedom hall
        Great women of Israel
        High school
        If not even higher
        Little learning (A)
        Magic top
        Magician
        Modern Modin
        Parting at Imsdorf

LESSON

Lesson (The)

LIARS

Liar's club
Willie's lie detector

LIGHT

And there was light

LIGHTHOUSE

Light on Tern Rock

LINCOLN

Abraham Lincoln
Ann Rutledge
Be not afraid
Boy Abe
Champions of democracy
China-handled knife
Lawyer Lincoln
Medal for Miss Walker
Mr. Lincoln's beard
Nor long remember
Shirt-tail boy
Sing the songs of Lincoln

LINCOLN'S BIRTHDAY

Abe Lincoln & little Joe
Abe Lincoln goes to school
Abe Lincoln in Illinois
G for Gettysburg
Gifts for young Abe
Man like Lincoln
Melody for Lincoln
Mystery of Knob Creek farm
Present for Abe
Ten pennies for Lincoln
Young Abe Lincoln

LONELINESS

Incident at Standish Arms
Touch of marble
White butterfly

LOVE

Italian love song
Jet of blood
Love
Love's labor
Mall (The)

LUMBERING

Giant of the timber

LUNCH ROOM

Hot off the griddle

LYNCHING

Judge Lynch

MAGIC

Eliza & the lexicon
Juan & the magic fruit
Magic box
Magic well
Tragical history of Dr. Faustus

MAN

Proof of a man

MATHEMATICS

Count of donkey's island

MATRIMONY

Bachelor husbands
Cecile
Half an hour
Here we are
His & hers
In the shadow of the glen
Lavender kite
Miss Julie
Proposal
That's different
Ugly duckling
Under plain cover
Woman's privilege

MEDICINE

Dr Killemquick's medicine show
Elizabeth Blackwell—pioneer woman
So precious a gift

MEDIEVAL LIFE

Border raid
Get up and bar the door
Johan, Johan
Queen Puff-puff

MELODRAMA

Mind of a killer
No no a thousand times no!
Steps from beyond

MEMORIAL DAY

Forward march
Lacey's last garland
Memorial day for the blue & the gray
Nor long remember
Part-time hero
Portrait of an American
Teddy bear hero

MEMORY

Glass menagerie
Memory course

MIME

Act without words I
Act without words II

MINING

Edge o'dark
Hewers of coal
Sealing the compact
Short cut

MINORITIES

Minority of millions

MISER

Interlude

MISTRESS—SERVANT

Other tomorrows

MODERNIZATION

Let's modernize

MONASTERY

Port-Royal

MONEY

Adam's rib hurts
Finders keepers
Susie

MORTGAGE

Mary Anne's mortgage

MORTUARY

Boy in the basement

MOTHER-DAUGHTER

Bright is tomorrow
Day after forever

MOTHER GOOSE

Mother Goose bakeshop
Mother Goose's magic cookies
Old woman & her pig

MOTHERS DAY

All the world loves a mother
Coach (The)
Dial M for mother
Famous families
Gift twice given
Golden bell for mother
It's tough on mother
Life for mother
Lucky piece for mother
Magic carpet sweeper
Making mother over
May day for mother
Merry-go-round for mother

Mom's perfect day
Mother beats the band
Mothering Miss Mittie
Mother's admirers
Mother's fairy godmother
Mother's hidden talent
Mother's V I P's
Roses for mother
Second Sunday in May
Violets for mother's day
We want mother
What gold cannot buy
Your mom & my mom

MOVING PICTURE

Colossal, stupendous!
Hollywood horseplay
Movie man (The)
Star dust

MURDER

Monster (The)
Roof (The)
Sheriff (The)

MUSIC

Blue concerto
Harmony a la hobo
Meeting to music
Melody man
Music—cure
Tenor (The)

MUSEUM

Astonishing Mrs. O'Shaugnessey

MYSTERY

Anonymous letter
Behold the body
Cynthia
Eenie, meenie, minee, murder
New neighbor
Mystery manor
Room upstairs
Shall we join the ladies

PAINTING

Painting (The)
Portrait (The)

PARENTS NIGHT

Crossroads to Education
Mrs. Bates at the PTA
Plenty of rein

PEACE

All quiet in the air
Answer (The)
Door was closed
Eleventh hour
Governor (The)
Great choice
Jonathan's day
Last war
Not this man
On the frontier
Peace is an olive color
Pen is mightier

PEDDLERS

Prince of peddlers
Yankee peddler

PENITENTIARY

This dark world & wide

PEOPLE

People with light coming out of them

PERSONAL RELATIONS

You'd never think it

PHOTOGRAPHY

Comrades in arms
Watch the birdies

PICNIC

Antic spring
It's no picnic

PICTURE

Just a picture

PIE

Blackberry pie

PIERROT

Maker of dreams

PILGRIMS

Return of the Pilgrims

PIRATES

Corsair
Pirate king
Runaway pirate
Under the skull & bones

PIXIE

Pixie in a trap

PLANE WRECK

Cup of strength

PLAY (STAGING)

Impromptu
Lemon curd

POETIC

Fall of the city
Really significant poem

POISON

Poison ivy

POLICEMEN

I want a policeman

POLITICS

Aloysius bigmouth

PULLMAN CAR

Pullman car Hiawatha

PUNCTUATION

Sound punctuation

PUPPETS

Betty & her friends
Betty's birthday
Betty's surprise
City mouse & the country mouse
David's rabbits
Dog for Betty
Goldilocks & the three bears
King Midas & the golden touch
Little bear tries to see Santa Claus
Little red hen
Little Red Riding Hood
Mother hen
Mummy's secret
Pirates chest
Princess who couldn't cry
Rainy day
Shakes versus Shav
Story of Christmas
Three bears
Three billy goats Gruff
Three little pigs

PUSH

Gentle push

QUARANTINE

Four in a town

QUEENS

Alice in Queenland

QUESTIONS

Why, daddy?

QUIZ PROGRAMS

Inconsequential journeys
Musical answers

Bible—New Testament
Christ

    And he came to his father
    Arrest in the garden
    Ascension
    Baptism of Jesus
    Boyhood of Jesus
    Calling of the disciples
    Centurion's servant
    Child is born
    Christ enters Jerusalem
    Christ the son of God
    Cristo (El)
    Cleansing of the temple
    Death of Jesus & the resurrection
    First breakfast
    Gift of the holy spirit
    Healing at the pool of Bethsheba
    Healing of the man born blind
    Healing of the paralyzed man
    Herod & the magi
    Jesus appears in Galilee
    Jesus appears to His disciples
    Jesus returns to Galilee
    Journey to Jerusalem
    Last supper
    Living dramatization of the Beatitudes
    Lord's prayer
    Martha & Mary
    Nativity
    Near calvary
    Parable of the last judgment
    Parable of the Pharisee & the tax collector
    Resurrection of Jesus
    Temptation of Jesus
    Transfiguration
    Trial before Pilate

Religous

    All in a day's work
    All roads lead to Rome
    Case against Eve
    Certain Greeks
    Charity
    Children of the book
    Christ in Concrete City
    Circle beyond fear
    Curate's play
    Eternal life
    Eyes upon the cross
    Father Sullac's cabbages
    Fresh start for the Beales

Through prophecy
Through the holy spirit
Through wisdom
Through witnessing
Travellers
Verdict
Uncle Sam
Unwelcome vision
Wall (The)
We are witnesses
Week before his death
What child is this?
Whosoever believeth
Wise virgins & foolish virgins
Women at the well
Women in the kitchen
Word (The)
Young man of means
Zeal of thy house

Easter

Alabaster cruse
Asher, the camel boy
Bashful bunny
Baskets or bonnets
Be nice to the easter bunny
Boy who discovered easter
Bunnies or bonnets
Bunny of the year
Come down
Cross (The)
Faithless
For the time being
Hats & rabbits
He is risen
Holy experiment
Magic egg
On calvary, a garden
Peppermint easter egg
Prince of peace
Rabbits who changed their minds
Three faces of easter
White House rabbit

Medieval religous plays

Abraham & Isaac
Adam
Annunciation & conception
Ascension
Birth of Christ
Creation of man
Death in the tree
Fall of Lucifer

Fall of man
Garden of Eden
Harrowing of hell
Herod & the kings
Last judgment
Noah's flood
Palm Sunday
Play of St. George
Play of the shepherds
Sacrifice of Isaac
Second trial before Pilate
Second shepherd's play
Temptation of Christ
Three Maries
Woman taken in adultery
Miracle plays
St. Nicholas & the three scholars
Shepherds play
Statue of St. Nicholas
Missionary
African Queen
Come over to Macedonia
Go, ye faithful witnesses
Heathen prisoner
Money talks
Night of the hunter
Send the light
Small victory
Unto one of these
Who's for the divide?
Women to remember
Morality play
Castle of perseverance
Death of giant despair
Everyman
Last word

REST

Goodnight please
I'm not here

REST HOME

Rockers

RESTAURANT

Hot cakes
Not on the menu
Song of songs
Waiter who waited

REVENGE

Red peppers
Sweet revenge

ROAD

Stone in the road

ROMANCE

Boy meets family
Call me dear
Dear Lottie
Doctor decides
End it all
Entertaining sister's beaux
Going home from the dance
Help wanted
I love you, Mr. Klotz!
If thoughts could speak
Merry Mollie Malone
My fair Linda
Prince & the sleeping beauty
Sparkin'
Splint for a broken heart
Too much Mary Jane
Treasure at Bentley Inn
Three on a bench
Three's a crowd
Trysting place

ROOMING HOUSE

Survival

RUMMAGE SALE

And what a rummage sale

SAFETY WEEK

Knight of safety
Smokey wins his star

ST. PATRICK DAY

Light on Shane
Little lost leprechaun
Mrs. Murphy's chowder
Prize shamrock

St. Patrick
St. Patrick's eve

SALESMAN

Cicero the great
Free samples
High pressure
144 davenports
Smith brothers cough drops

SALOON

Johnny Aladdin

SCHOOL

All who enter
Browning version
Bow-wow blues
Burning schoolhouse
Cabana blues
District school at Carrot Corners
End of the term
Fast finish
How to study
Lesson
Mother's pet
Not for credit
Old village school
Perfect gentleman
Polly Patchwork
Printer's devil
Reason enough
Salvation of Lonny McCain
School days
School daze minstrels
Speeches & cream
Ten-penny tragedy
Time machine
What a classroom!
Worming around

SEA

Embers

SCIENCE

Anyone for the moon?
Anywhere & everywhere
Catastrophe Clarence

Day the moon men landed
First cat on Mars
Ghost from outer space
Invasion from the stratosphere
Little man who wasn't there
Madame Curie
Miss Tarzen into space
Moon's up there
Mouse that soared
Pinky Windy's trip to the moon
Science is wonderful
U F O
Visit to a small planet
Visitor from outer space

SECRET

Something unspoken

SENTIMENT

Sentimental scarecrow

SERVICE

How to put them on

SEX

Overruled
Stronger sex

SHIPS

Shipmates
Shiver my timbers
Thirst
Warnings
What's in a name?

SHIRT

Shirt's off

SHOW-OFF

Poor Aubrey

SIGNPOSTS

Signpost

SPRING

Mother Earth's new dress
Ode to spring
Planting time
Sing the songs of springtime
Spring daze

STAGE

Property man

STATISTICS

Statistics

STOCK YARDS

Saint Joan of the stock yards

STRIKE

Strike (The)

SUBSCRIPTION

Subscribe now

SUICIDE

Too close for comfort

SUITOR

Enter the hero

SUMMER

Memory of summer

SUNSTROKE

Sunstroke

SUPERMARKET

Vote for Miss Checkout
We deliver most anywhere

SUPERSTITION

Living dead man
Monkey's paw
That's the spirit

SURREALISM

Chairs (The)

SUSPENSE

Beware, Miss Brown, beware
Red key
You're a long time dead

TAVERN

For want of character
Sight for sore thoughts

TAXES

Battle of the budget
Income tax
Outcome of income

TEEN AGERS

"Don't call me Junior"
Double date
First dress suit
Five for bad luck
Forever Judy
His first date
Love errant
Pinina goes to Hollywood
Puzzle (The)
Rented tux
Sugar & spice
Teen-age party

TEETH

King's toothache

TELEPATHY

Professor Cookoo, crystal gazer

TELEPHONE

Cards on the table
Sorry, wrong number
Wire trouble

TELEVISION

Adventures of Ozzie & Harriet
Bob Cummings show
Evening bells
Garry Moore show
Goldbergs
Jack Benny program
Jack Paar show
Life of Riley
Make room for Daddy
Martha Raye show
People to people
Perry Como show
Ripe strawberries

THANKSGIVING

ABC's Thanksgiving
Bartholomew's joyful noise
Day of thanks
Dinner with the folks
Everyday is Thanksgiving
Broadway turkey
First Thanksgiving
Horn of plenty
If we could only cook
Jimmy & the same old stuff
Jonathan's Thanksgiving
Mr. Snow White's Thanksgiving
Mystery of Turkey-Lurkey
Pilgrim Thanksgiving service
Sing the songs of Thanksgiving
Strictly Puritan
Thankful's red beads
Thanks for Thanksgiving
Thanks to butter-finger
Thanksgiving a la carte
Thanksgiving eve
Thanksgiving postscript
Thanksgiving riddle
Thanksgiving with Uncle Sam
Too much turkey
What, no venison?

TRAVEL

Albuquerque ten minutes
Mrs. Wickens in the fall
Romance
Sing the songs of travel
This is New York
Traveler (The)

TRIAL

Amorous goldfish
One in twelve

TRIANGLE

Astonished heart
For distinguished service
How he lied to her husband
Recklessness
Two's company
We were dancing

TRIFLES

Trifles

TROUBLE

Box of trouble

TRUTH

Simple truth

TURNCOAT

Turncoat

TURNING POINT

Turning point

UMBRELLAS

Umbrellas

UNION

In union

UNITED NATIONS

Accident of birth
Alice in Puzzleland
All in the U N
All the world around
Best bargain in the world
Cavalcade of human rights
Empty bowls
Food for freedom
Fresco for Inesco
Get together dinner
Getting in line
Invasion of the stratosphere
Let there be bread
Nickel & a dime
Of gods & men
Program for peace
Skills to share
Story of a well
Thanks a million
Turning the tables
What happened in Egypt

UNIVERSITY

Long view

UNIVERSE

Leak in the universe

URBAN

Hour of honor

VALENTINE DAY

Crosspatch & cupid
Cupid & Co.
Happy Valentine day
Heart trouble
Kindly heart
Princess Lonely Heart
St. Valentine's surprise
Shower of hearts
Somebody's valentine
Stolen heart
To my Valentine
Tree of hearts
Valentine box

Valentine for Kate
Valentine sale

VAUDEVILLE

Home life of a buffalo
Kitchen kanaries
Voice from nowhere

VETERANS' DAY

Forgotten hero
Keys to peace
Over the years
Soldiers of peace
Stage set for Veteran's day

VISITORS

Hands across the sea

VOTES

Anything to get votes
Sample ballot

WALL

Other side of the wall

WASHINGTON'S BIRTHDAY

At the bend of the road
Bake a cherry pie
Call Washington 1776
Dolly saves the day
Echo of '76
Enter, George Washington
First in peace
General Gage's chowder
General George
General returns
Imaginary trial of George Washington
Let George do it
New Washington
Visit from Washington
Washington shilling
Washington's gold button
Washington's leading lady

WOMANS CLUB

Charmed, I'm sure
Fat woman
For women only
Green room blues
In union
Just made it
Lay this body down
Seven women
Twelve pound look
Two women

WONDERS

Susie wonders

WOOING

Village wooing

WORD

Slight misunderstanding

WORK

Heavy chiffonier

WORKHOUSE

Workhouse ward

WORLD

It might happen
Out of this world

SUBJECT INDEX

A

Accidents
Acting
Actors
Actresses
Adaptations
    Alcott
    Andersen
    Arabian nights
    Atwater
    Baum
    Bible
    Bunyan
    Burnett
    Carroll
    Cervantes
    Chaucer
    Dickens
    Doyle
    Dumas
    Field
    Graham
    Greek myths
    Grimm
    Hardy
    Hawthorne
    Homer
    Hope
    Howells
    Hugo
    Irving
    King Arthur
    Lang
    Mark Twain

    Moliere
    Poe
    Pyle
    Sachs
    Scott
    Shakespeare
    Sheridan
    Swift
    Thurber
    Tolstoi
    Verne
    Wilde
    Wyss
Adventure
Adolescents
Affairs
Airplane
Alchemist
Alcoholism
Allegory
Animals
Antiques
Apartment life
April Fool day
Arrival
Art
Artist
Astronomy
Athletics
Atomic
Auction
Autograph
Automobile

B

Baby
Baby sitter
Backwoods
Bake contest
Ball
Balloon
Bank
Barber
Baseball

Be kind to animals week
Beatnicks
Beauty
Beggars
Biography
    Jane Addams
    Appleseed
    Benedict Arnold
    John J. Astor

C

I

Ideas
Imagination
Impersonation
Imposters
Income tax
Indian life

Insane asylum
Insects
Intrigue
Inventions
Invitation
Islands

J

Jealousy
Jews—Holidays
    Canukah
    Kol Nidre
    Passover
    Purim
    Rosh Hashana

    Shavuot
    Sukkot
Jews—life & culture
Jobs for girls
Junk
Justice
Juvenile delinquency

L

Labor
Latin
Laughter
Lawyers
Legacy
Legends
Lesson
Liars
Light

Lighthouse
Lincoln
Lincoln's birthday
Loneliness
Love
Lumbering
Lunch room
Lynching

M

Magic
Man
Mathematics
Matrimony
Medicine
Medieval life
Melodrama
Memorial day
Memory
Mime
Mining
Minorities
Miser

Mistress-servant
Modernize
Monastery
Money
Mortgage
Mortuary
Mother Goose
Mothers day
Moving pictures
Murder
Music
Museum
Mystery

N

Nature
Negro
New Americans day

New Years day
Newly rich

S

Safety week
St. Patrick day
Salesman
Saloon
School
Sea
Science
Secret
Sentiment
Service
Sex
Ships
Shirt
Show-off
Signpost
Silence
Skit
Smell
Soap box derby

Social climbing
Soda fountain
Sorority house
Spelling
Spirits
Spring
Stage
Statistics
Stockyards
Strike
Subscriptions
Suicide
Summer
Sunstroke
Supermarket
Superstition
Surrealism
Suspense

T

Tavern
Taxes
Teen agers
Teeth
Telepathy
Telephone
Television
Thanksgiving day
Theatre
Thieves
Time
Tolerance
Toys

Tractor
Tragedy
Train
Tramp steamer
Travel
Trial
Triangle
Trifles
Trouble
Truth
Turncoat
Turning point

U

Umbrellas
Union
United Nations

University
Universe
Urban

V

Valentine day
Vaudeville
Veterans' day

Visitors
Votes

W